The Soul's Journey to Love
Book Two

THE DIVINE
SENSES

Valentina M. Grosvenor

DISCLAIMER

The information within this book is given in good faith, received from a source outside of the author, and is considered spiritual advice relating to life's issues. It is not intended to diagnose any physical or mental condition nor to serve as a substitute for informed medical advice or care. Please contact a competent health professional if assistance or counseling is needed. If you are experiencing urgent spiritual issues and distress, consult a practitioner with an awareness and competency in spiritual emergence and spiritual emergencies.

The author cannot be held liable by any person for any loss or damage whatsoever which may arise from the use of this book or any of the information therein.

Books in this Series

by Valentina M. Grosvenor

Book One: The Soul's Journey to Love

Book Two: The Divine Senses

Book Three: Self-Care for the Weary Soul

Book Four: Entitlement to Your Birthright

Book Five: The Welcoming Home

Contents

Dear Humanity,

Let there be light upon the Soul.

Acknowledgements

Thank you Source, God, the All That Is, for the words that flowed, your wisdom, truth, and the gifts you have bestowed in me.

To my spiritual family for healing, teaching, and grounding me and my gifts in this physical world.

To my spirit guides, angels, and ancestors for guiding me each day. Your presence is a gift.

Finally, to my family and friends for surrounding me with love and believing in me through my hardest times.

Preface

by Valentina M. Grosvenor

The sharing of experiences is essential to understanding each other and that of the whole. Where one begins and ends their journey may not be the same as another, there are similar pain points that can be learned from, techniques that are known to some but most needed by others. In this way, a community is formed to harness the individual strengths for benefit of the whole.

Senses have a tendency to change over time and are influenced by the changes in our environment. Sensitivities come when we lack a connection to our own sensing abilities, thus predisposing us to symptoms that block or aggravate what is not functioning correctly. For me, this began as an extreme sensitivity to what was not right in my external world. A profession that no longer fit, an employer that did not value the skills I brought to the table, a marriage that no longer filled the deep cavity of my spirit that had lacked nourishment for so long.

To begin excavating required the push by my senses. They expanded enormously. From claircognizance, to clairvoyance and clairaudience–I was hearing, seeing, and feeling things that were far beyond my scope of existence. In my periphery was the sense that things were changing around me, but what I did not heed soon enough was that *I* was changing. I was evolving into something I never knew was possible.

Claires are within all of us, the deeper senses that exist when we are born and learn to suppress over time out of a lack of acceptance and inferiority. They become imagination, yet they hold the key for our insight into ourselves and the whole world around us.

Channeling is one of those insights, where access to information is granted to those who are willing to listen and lead the way back to these impeccable traits of ours. As human beings we have the benefit of intelligence, but what use is it if we cannot hear, smell, or see accurately? Accuracy comes with all aspects of information held by the source of the energy created. Rather than filtering this energy through our five physical senses, we see the energy from where it came, in its full form. From here, a response, action, or invitation to something most appropriate can be made.

Living with these changes can be daunting. It hurts, it pulls, it veers you in different directions because it is trying to get your attention for something important. Something Grand. Be still. Be receptive. Be willing to flow with the magic that is trying to unfold. Your brilliance, your beauty, your genuine perfection and willingness to see the world through all aspects of who you are: spirit, physical, emotional and mental bodies all functioning as one. Harmonious, intelligent, evolutionary beings we are.

Allow that to make its way to you, as you were created, as you were genuinely built in perfect form. To be yourself, purely, unabashedly. Become from within again so you can be the world that is waiting for your wonderous beauty. Believe and you shall become that which you are.

Greatness comes from within. Recall the many powerful creators that came from impoverished upbringings. The Soul has this in motion. Allow for it, allow for the All That Is to work from within, perfecting perfection in every sense of the way. Being it, creating it, loosening its grip over the way in which things "should" be. We are a mere reflection of our own capacity to dream. Dream big. It's already there waiting for you to step into. The magic is waiting for you to see that it exists here for you, in all its forms.

Aligning with this dream is merely a breath away, in stillness and centering we find it. We listen. We trust. We believe. And then, like a miraculous butterfly it emerges. Gently, transformed, transforming still, until its wings are ready to fly.

Introduction

There comes a time when we can no longer fear what is taking place–of us, around us–we can no longer say that it doesn't exist when it pervades every aspect of our being. Truth has a way of coming to the fore, when and where we need it. It resides deep in our core begging to come out. Daring to come out and see what the world can do with it, whether it has learned its auspicious ways. The intire need for it to come to the foreground is immense. It determines its course well before we know its attempts to destroy or deteriorate our ego, for it [ego] holds truth back under the auspices of knowing better than *It*, the truth.

The truth only knows one way, however. And it speaks in gentlest of terms with our soul in its attempts to be seen. First as a knowing, then a collection of signs and synchronicity, then a blowing wind which must be held onto for it will blow the socks off all those around you. It speaks in terms of guidance, of sensory abilities, of new and old systems throughout our body, our mind, our emotions. It can wreak havoc if we do not drop in deep into this place of knowing and sense what is being asked of us.

What must be done with this truth that we hold onto so tightly yet all it wants is to be seen, heard, embraced by all the earthly children that he has placed here to learn, to see with their own eyes, touch with their new capabilities. They know not yet what they do not know. Some will never hold the beauty in their hands to experience. Others may only reconcile parts of their truth in this lifetime. Whereas others will be the light holders of the way forward, of the way things must be in order for the trajectory to change the course of our demise.

We can no longer sit and revel in the material world in which we have built. We must move forward in our knowingness, trusting in the unseen for which we long to see, and establish a comfort in the love and grace that surrounds us at all times. For we are here to learn from this experience *and* bring about change to our fellow children and future generations. They hold the key to fostering the new world. We have the keys to open the door to it.

We can change once we have arrived or we can hold onto the way things were. There will be a struggle when we hold onto something that is no longer true or resonating with our world or the direction we, and the earth, need to move towards. It is a resistance that festers and brings the collective consciousness down towards a place of chaos or unrest. When we move the needle forward, we can feel palpably the quietness, peace that comes with non-resistance and harmony. It is a place, a pace, and forward motion we must keep striving for in order to reach individual and collective harmony.

On the global and universal scale this quietens the unrest felt in many places of the world while rejuvenating others. A balance that is impressed energetically, within our consciousness, and allowing for new growth to occur in the comfort of our resting and allowing for joy to return upon us. *This* is the natural state of growth and joy of being human, not in the consequences of our demise. To move forward continuously, ever so slightly by the directions given to us by our innermost seeing and knowing functions. It is there for us, guiding our way ever so slightly.

Now, let's dive deep into how this magic truly happens. Awaken your senses, awaken the possibilities, open your heart to a grander purpose of your true nature. At the heart of it all is evolution. No matter how challenging you feel your experiences are, they are leading you to truth. To love. To Source. And your everlasting love.

Chapter 1
Energy Speaks

This chapter is devoted to the senses that which the divine speaks through. That which we cannot see but is inextricably linked to our internal senses laying dormant within us until we are ready to see the unseen. Readiness is described as "the willingness to open our hearts to something beyond ourselves, beyond the logic of our minds and resting within this place in pure anticipation". This requires an awareness, an appreciation, and a curiosity for something more, to soothe our longing to go back home to ourselves. There are periods of readiness during the ascension process but only when this is sustained can it open to full capacity.

There is only one way in which the divine speaks—through energetic patterns and waves. The ability to perceive and decode the meaning of these is inherently existing within but is suppressed during our periods of learning so as not to overwhelm the body and cause anguish to the mind. Some individuals become ready sooner than others due to their pureness, an untethered nature of their soul, or a limitless belief system. Their bodies are less impacted by traumas that reduce the ability of the body to absorb the higher frequencies of the divine.

Being a divine being capable of receiving source codes is our innate nature. What is not innate is the tendency for beings to be caught up in the illusion of earthly existence–power, material goods, societies–that dictate our level of beingness. There comes a time when certain beings are called out of the matrix and into a life of knowing, being, and spiritual aspects. The level that can be attained is dependent only on the commitment one has towards self and Source.

How long it takes to achieve a direct connection with Source depends on the nature of traumas, age of the soul (and thus historical traumas), and the environment within which it is able to grow. The current environments and pace of life stifle the potential to quickly and smoothly enter the space of divine. It requires often, a detachment from daily life to foster and nurture presence with self such that all else falls away and incoming light has the opportunity to be perceived, felt, seen in all its glory. One moment at a time of this detachment will allow growth in this space.

Continued ignorance of all that is and all that can be will lead to disease of some sort, the severity based upon the willingness to soften, open, and look beyond ourselves. Victimhood is the most severe form of ignorance of our own powers that wish to manifest within us.

Ignoring our potential stifles the growth of families, communities, and the earth at large, where the power is seen as inconsequential, lacking, or merely nonexistent. Heaven-sent miracles may once in a while form a path for certain individuals who have destinies that must be contractually filled. But for the most part, the work is ours to acknowledge and recognize, foster, and follow through with.

A level of curiosity enables the body and mind to soften in a childlike way. Open to possibilities, not threatened by how we may be perceived, and challenged only by the barriers that we place upon ourselves. The capacity to internalize the information seen is equally influenced by similar factors. In addition, our thought processes must take a back seat within the latter parts of ascension when the physical body becomes exhausted and is longing for more light. This is when thoughts are destructive, carrying negative energy and spiraling the mind into an abyss.

The key to letting our thoughts go from the power of self-rumination is to acknowledge the underlying meaning and then disposing of it in some form. This can be through meditation, visualization, or sacred burning. Exiting the body is of importance, as with any negative energy that comes within our sphere. There can be no curiosity when there is unwillingness to detach from the stories we hold. A new way must be invited each and every day. Help is on its way at all times.

Are you open to receiving it?

If a novel solution was presented to you, would you open that gift or dismiss it as fringe and disbelieve?

What would the world look like if we were more open to receiving, to being, to trying that which seems illogical but is rooted in the intricacies that the earth has laid out in front of us in countless ways?

We underestimate this power because we have no proof, yet there is proof everywhere. From the way in which birds can communicate without sound, the ocean's ability to transmit across vast distances. So is the power within each of us. Purely in sync, functioning with or without our mental desires, living, breathing, nourishing, one cell at a time, within a system of systems.

We can all recall a time when we have been stupefied from an occurrence. Not knowing how but knowing its trueness. This is where we must reside on a day-to-day for our abilities to be harnessed, utilized, and to receive more. **When we do not doubt our power, we are gifted more and more and more. It is limitless.** The desire of course must be utilized based on pure intention, as was discussed in Book One. From this place, manifesting greatness is the destiny we are all here for.

The power of energy within and around us can be seen as a reciprocal exchange, sharing, giving, receiving. To the earth, to beings, to the forest, and back again. There is an evolution to this energy rather than an end or beginning. It ceases to exist only when the fire of our heart and soul reaches its endpoint in this realm, in this reincarnation. The energy forces begin again once we have gathered enough strength in the spiritual dimension for a return and attempt to relearn our destiny.

There is only light upon our departure that carries us to other worlds to wait on our return. The exchange of energy we speak of is that of sound and sight, the slightest reverberations can be felt within the inner ear messaging our brain to be alert for more information. This sends a notice to our vision centers—the third eye and the ventricles–to become attuned to the impending sensory information.

There is a minor amount of information that is received by the physical eyes, cornea, and visual cortex; thus, what we see within our vision is only a fraction of the story as a whole. The picture we portray in our field of vision marks only the starting point of what exists to be told and learned from our surroundings. The mental image is further reduced by our mental mapping and reframing of our conscious thought around what we see. The field of energy is large and thus our perception and reaction to this limited sphere of vision is the source of great suffering.

Where there is sound, there are waves. Where there are waves there is a flow of information from the source of the wave. Herein lays the fullest source of knowledge and truth. Achieving and gaining the fullest perspective requires reaching that source point, receiving all packets of information in all aspects. The mind must be still for this to occur fully, training the reactionary aspects of the human mind to cease and only respond once all aspects of information are received.

The source will never lie.

The source is the origin of truth.

The physical body surrounding that source may not even be aware or awake to its own truth, thereby externalizing and projecting what it feels to be the message based on their own conditioning and belief systems. For the messages of source to be truly understood and 'heard' by both beings is a never-ending challenge, for no two beings will be at the same point of awareness at the same time.

This fluctuation between full-knowing and half-knowing is the source of relationship confusion, wars, and controversies, where one does not know their own truth and source of action towards another. The motivation is obscured, the result, is a tension on an energetic level between the awake and unawakened.

Chapter 2
Diamonds are Born from Pressure

As a diamond forms from the basic elements of silica dust[1], so is our greatness. The basics must be present in its purest form. The pressure that makes a real diamond is the same pressure that results in human greatness, a perseverance to withstand at all cost, for there is known to be a great outcome.

The earth knows this–it is how we were built–in the same way a diamond is built. The pressure is not meant to harm or hinder us. **When we relax into the pressure and allow the energy to make its magic, we fall away from ourselves and what stands in its way.** We are pure magic at our core.

The fine particles that make up the diamond are the same elements that are housed within the physical body. There are elements that do more than others, but they all serve a purpose–to form something beyond what we are. The pressure element of the process does not begin until the conditions are ripe for building, similar to that of the diamond. Heat exchange, the buildup, all

---

1. References to some scientific terms, theories or systems are described out of familiarity not of accuracy in order to assist us in seeing the overarching context and point being made.

must be in perfect timing. Where there is a will to allow for the human process to *be*, this is when the conditions are allowing the next stages to form, a momentum, each stage building upon the previous.

A marked acceleration occurs when the pressure to *be* is more than the pressure to *do*, an oxymoron, considering our [human] definition of doing includes exerting effort, energy, and activity. The former simply requires silence, serenity, and a complete openness to being worked through and not to be the doer.

The Universe conspires to build greatness and cannot do so if there is a competing force against it. There is intention for greatness already, we do not need to create more of what is already destined. *Just be the destined.* Be it until it presents itself in front of you before your very eyes. It will form. It is the Universes' predetermined form of art that comes into view. The image changes as it forms, but that is the beauty of becoming what is destined.

There lies a truth to a diamond that most cannot see. Only the finely tuned can observe the facets that form under this beautiful area of energy, pressing each particle against each other until they shift shapes, changing form, changing in structure and luminosity. The luminosity is a function of continuous pressure, withstanding the propensity to release or relieve through some opening or crack. The surrounding environment, if pure and free of cracks, will serve the diamond well. **The presence of cracks does not result in a diamond of less beauty, rather reveals beauty even where the conditions fail to achieve perfection. This is the beauty**

of life. We are all of beauty regardless of cracks and imperfections and each can thrive despite the conditions around us.

All of our anxieties serve to pressurize us out of the state of doing towards a state of being. When the pressure is too hot, we will surrender if we know what is best for us and our path to greatness. Shifts in environment are done for our benefit, in either direction to move us out of a state that no longer serves us. If we're nudged each and every day we may not notice. When we are shoved, we notice but we may not act.

When we are forced in a different direction, we are made to see what has been in our blind spots the whole time. It is these blind spots–aha moments–that can wake us for good, but they must be strong enough to overcome our desire for stability and the need to know. For if we had comfort in the unknowns, we would have seen them all along as mere options, opportunities rather than an abyss to be fallen into.

How many times have we failed to take a risk simply because there was information missing and the picture not perfectly clear?

How many times have we failed to take that opportunity because we did not feel deserving or as beautiful as someone else?

These are gaps in our trust and faith in the Universe for it to provide for us everything we need and desire in each moment. Instead of believing it is conspiring for us, we believe it conspires against us. And so, we move in the opposite direction of that which calls us in.

We can either choose to align with the Universe or fight it. If we refuse to look at what is staring us in the face, we progressively burn ourselves out from the effort it takes in avoidance. When we turn to stare back, we allow it to envelope us, embrace us, nurture us from within and from without. There is nothing to do but rest. Rest in the knowing that we are cared for amongst all things for our best and highest good. At all times.

We may face occasional obstacles, but these are also strategically placed to test our commitment to standing firm in our place with Universe. Braced and confident in ourselves and what upholds our very existence. There can be no faltering when there is this level of trust in a greater unseen force that conspires for us, because we are all deserving of such unwavering love from God Source.

Unimaginable to the human mind is there something such as this, as it contradicts our whole system of values and beliefs in society. That there is no one completely capable of benevolence. There is a belief that all beings serve their own needs and desires first at some level. Hierarchy and power cannot be nonexistent. There must always be an order to civilization, and no one is absolved of these structures.

Unless we move beyond this paradigm in our civilization there will always be competition. But what Universe is aiming for is our collective acknowledgment that there does not need to be competition. That we are all provided for; therefore, competing over power, food, goods, status, is simply a waste of our life force. Our life force is meant to serve us not be drained from us by perpetual doing. Even where those feel they are "powered up" by doing, this is simply a fallacy because ultimately, they are drawing from the life forces of those that surround them. Unless their power is generated through earthing.

The first step in the process of pressurizing is that of acknowledgement, that where you are does not serve your fullest potential. Surrender to that. It is not a failure to achieve, it is simply the wrong placement for you. It drew you there to be seen. And by seeing you get to choose your way out of where you are and towards a better placement. This is not an act of doing, rather a beingness of acceptance. Your next choices may require you to act, however, this is propelled by the beingness. Not the other way around.

The next steps are laid out for you brick by brick, not as a full picture or map so to speak. It is in this process that we are building our capacity to trust–in the absence of the full picture–we are willing to take one step at a time as it is presented to us, not rushing, simply being aware and acknowledging what is best for our path from one moment to another. This trust lays the foundation for everything else to come our way.

Conspiring for us takes time. From moving parts, people, places, choices you make that are in opposing directions, requires constant course corrections behind the scenes. It is no wonder that what we seem to try and trust, feels like an eternity to arrive. **What we are manifesting is greater than we can see, beyond our own imagination, therefore leaving the design of our destiny to the expertise of the Universe is essential.** Taking it into our hands will certainly delay it more.

Then what is the notion of co-creating if we cannot actually take part in the design?

Are we not simply letting the wind carry us like a leaf, aimlessly?

There is a difference in the allowing of our destiny through creating an environment that is conducive to our being, space to thrive, to allow what comes. This is our role in the creation. It is not hands-off by any means. It is the intentional allowing, feeling, being, releasing all that which was hindering us to that point in time. It is not aimless, not floating, not without direction. It is the boat that is well-maintained to prevent leaks, withstand the pressure of the water and wind that comes upon us, and maintaining or aligning our direction to our true north. We are the boat that gets our self there. Our boat requires a constant presence, upkeep, and caring for such that we can be carried wholly and meticulously to our destination. To keep watch at all times is to care for, nurture, and trust that we can withstand the most severe of storms that come our way.

So, what do boats and diamonds have in common? A beauty, a journey, a process. A trust in its surroundings and a trust in its captain.

For where would we be without trust?

Where would we be without constant nurturing and self-care?

We would not be able to withstand the pressure that arrives to us as part of our journey home. Our journey home is meant to be of learning, of challenge, of falling and getting up again. From each challenge, we learn more of what we are capable of, more faith, more trust in the unseen, and in the glory of making it through to the other side. A willingness to keep going, because we survived many times before.

Chapter 3
The Knowing

Naturally, there is an inclination to receive only what the mind perceives to be of interest or use to its limited scope of view. What happens when we expand our view beyond the five senses is we gain access to magical parts of the Universe that were not readily available to us.

There is a quality to the energy that is easily overlooked in our rugged view of life. Seemingly innocent and unapparent compared to the dense, heavy weight of the others. A quality that is nearly imperceptible to the naked eye and ear. A resonance that can only be felt by the heart. This is the Knowing. The pulse is fine, gentle, in a range that only babies hear in their first few days of birth. The pattern between embryo and mother, a pulse so fine yet finite as the density of the earth plane surrounds the new being. This is innate to humans, yet our lives created a habit of drowning it away.

All is not lost for those who awake to these senses. They do come back, they do have purpose, they do have meaning within ourselves and amongst those who cherish and nurture their souls back to health. The length and quality endured during the state of unconscious living will determine the strength and power of this sense, along with the true purpose behind the soul. Those whose purpose is to rebuild society will have their innate sense returned to them without change, for they will and must execute their purpose in this lifetime.

For others, there is time in this life and next to hone the skill and tune ever so slightly without bearing the weight of their full evolution all at once. There comes a time when all beings will be pushed into accepting what has been rightly theirs all along.

What you do with the sense varies with the skills and gifts you have inherited. They will draw out and draw upon these gifts at different stages of the life course, at the right time and place. Where there is visibility and awareness of gifts and a full acceptance of these, there will be mutual reliance for growth and survival. There is no longer a benefit of the usual human devotion to work for the purpose of maintaining a lifestyle. There is a renewed passion for simply the art of breathing, of listening, of watching. There is no greater purpose of the day-to-day meandering of one's life course. It is the life course to simply *be*.

How might you ask would one make a living and feed their family? By way of harnessing energy within their sphere or locus of control, for the pure purpose of serving others. Where others are deemed to be mutually exchanging energy in return for service, there will be a return. Like attracts like. And wealth comes from the heart of being.

Surrounding oneself with beings of like minds have no need to barter, negotiate, or pay. There is a natural return on the service provided, whether monetary, service, sustenance, or otherwise.

There is a different system at play—one of mutual regard and respect, of equitable place in society. There is no hierarchy. All have what they need.

Where there is a need, the Knowing will draw you there. This will present initially as a pulse from Spirit, of the hands, a transmission elsewhere sending what information needs to be relayed. This will happen spontaneously, often unknowingly, and without context to what, who, or why. Trust the Knowing. It goes where it is needed and meant to be. It is the power of the heart and soul to move past the mind and ego's preoccupation with status and return.

There is no need to know what the Knowing is doing or manifesting on your behalf. There is a trueness that is dulled when you interfere with its work. The only doing required as a human is to remain in a state of being. There is nothing to do. Help will be provided only when there is distress on the other side that is beyond your expertise. Where there is passion to remain in and foster this exchange, returns are amplified immeasurably. Where there is faith there is ease. No requirements for efforting. Just be.

Enlivening the spirit is beneficial through joyous activities and pursuits; these fulfill and nourish, but are not required for success in using and fostering the Knowing. Even the most dreary of persons can successfully embrace and maintain this state of being. Joy merely packages the experience differently and may be necessary for those who have a tendency for overdoing "humanness" and have a need for activity and high-energy doses. This is the ultimate in passion for one's own purpose and living the earthly realms to the fullest extent.

Be kind to the soul that seeks to retract from these busy activities, for there is usually a need and purpose to doing so, and which may be time-limited rather than never-ending. Search for souls who, like you, recognize the benefits of the new world and can foster an environment that serves you more easily.

Chapter 4
The Awakening

The process of awakening is merely like cracking an egg open to see the wonderous substance inside. The egg that carries life force so deep within that sometimes it remains hidden beneath the viscous albumin, clouding the view through to the wondrous golden yolk inside. Rich with nutrients, dense in power, and the ability to transform into life with the appropriate environmental conditions, harmony, and care.

There is a yoke within all of us that seeks to be seen, to be nourished under the warmth of the brilliant sun, cared for by the deep blue seas that rain down on the crevices of the earth. The crack in the shell is where it all starts. Breaking through the wall that is not of protection but of barrier to the greatness on each side.

The crack may be abrupt, or it may be slow and persistent. It is the crack that allows the light to shine through onto the possibility of something bigger and brighter inside of us. The story unfolds from here. Each of us born within a story to tell and a story to experience. This is not for the faint of heart. It is of intense pleasure and pain simultaneously, as we arrive home to ourselves and that which has been missing from our daily lives until then.

There is a wonder, a curiosity, a stillness, and peacefulness when you begin. An arrival to your beingness. The unfolding of years of hiding is where the pain lays, of being unseen, unforsaken, unknown to the presence that you say is you.

But, is it truly you?

Do you truly know you at each crevice and peak, at each turn of the emotions that arrive?

Do you know which one is you?

The dual nature of your being makes it easy to choose the side of you that hides. It is easier than facing the true you. The deeper you. For it is in the depths that we must face our demons and shadows–as if they are something outside of us, external, instead of being what they are. Part of us. And so, the extricated part of our being remains hurt, hidden, extricated from our mental selves to avoid feeling and seeing them. **We cannot heal what we cannot or are not willing to see.** The door has always been open, but few are willing to go there in the absence of an existential crisis.

The crisis becomes the disharmony within our spirit world. When spirit proclaims, "No More," the egg cracks. The pressure and consequences are too great. The time is decided for us and the choice is ours to either accept the path for what it is or return into our hiding to await the bigger crack to arrive. Some will say that they have no choice but to follow the path, for the force is so strong or incessantly present that avoiding is truly not an option. Others choose to bury their head in the sand, neglecting themselves further down a spiral into victimhood. Never seeing the brightness that is meant to come through. Hindered by the fear of stepping into themselves, literally and figuratively. **The strength must come from inside. From having faith in your true greatness and power to overcome all that comes your way.**

Step into yourself when the time comes. If the time has come and your fear holds you back, step into your fear in order to step into yourself. Fear is merely an illusion that you can walk through anytime to see the other side. You will find yourself there with no more reason to avoid yourself. Test this out for yourself whenever you are faced with the fear. You will find yourself on the other side each and every time. The purpose to awakening is to see this illusion and all others that surround us and drive our actions, behaviors, and emotions.

Much is driven out of habit and unconscious response to negative stimuli that is no wonder we have a society that cannot control their reckless behavior much less have a positive impact on society as a whole. In seeing this individually it is an opportunity to change the system from within, one at a time.

Relative change occurs by the amount of inner work we are willing to undertake, both on benefit to ourselves but also of benefit to the whole. Where one cannot see themselves as part of the whole there will be minimal impact. There is benefit still, of course, one step, one moment, which may simply be the timing that is required for certain individuals.

In the case of others, where the feeling of being thrown into the deep to sink or swim becomes the reality for years to come. Persistence is the key, following the internal compass at each and every step of the way. This internal guidance mechanism is set to intentionally reactivate at this time in the traditional sense that when we are truly ready, we will be guided by something bigger than us and with the ability to function through us at an individual level yet connected to the whole.

This bigger "thing" or Knowing as we have called it, is the Universes' way of returning to order, to harmony, and balance. Once we get past these awakenings and begin living within our brilliance we will not weaken. For our intentions on the earthly plane will be for mutual harmony and the dis-ease that we have become to know so well will not be an option. It will not exist under the guise of true balance and equality. That does not mean we will become immortal and free of age-related degeneration. What will change is our way of being and behavior such that our appreciation of greatness will be paramount over individual power. We are the sum of the whole at that point, the weight of greatness will exceed that of greed.

Walking through life in a new way will provide a reprieve to the energetic systems of the Universe, a rebalancing of all that lives. This will take a generation or two but will be foundational for planetary existence.

Returning to self becomes an integral component of the wholeness of all.

Chapter 5
The Chrysalis

The rewards of awakening can be equated to the blooming of a rose or the resurgence of the butterfly from its chrysalis pod. The period inside oneself can feel dark and dreary, but the colours abound once the growing is complete.

The efforts within do not go unnoticed. Step by step as you are guided down the path of enlightenment, your efforts and movements are recorded in the Akash wherein you will be rewarded in future stages of growth. Whether in finances, love, or joy, the abundance comes ten-fold for those who prepare themselves for the lengthy journey to serve humanity. The reward is not the goal however, for service is a reward in and of itself.

By and large, the rewards that come are to nurture you back to health such that your ability to give in service to others no longer becomes a barrier. It marks a new way for you to live, free from the shackles that prevented you from stepping into who you really are. The barriers that once were are no longer, easing you into the more fulsome and vibrant part of your journey.

The reward of persistence is unimaginable to the naked eye. It comes in the form of access to information that is unavailable to most. It is there for you to build your empire of service upon such that you are free to wander the earth with love, security, and peacefulness. A trust that is unwavering, infallible, unconditional to you specifically. There are merits in the Universe doing so, for it magnetizes more of the same, an ease to its inception and growth, magnifying the return on its investment. **It knows the cards that it is playing and feeds that which is playing its own game.**

Fostering safety is critical in a tumultuous and unclear path. Reigniting energy systems that may be depleted is a form of return on investment–∞, infinity–reciprocal in its nature, loving so that it may be loved. Our nature depends on this reciprocity and is willing to give more to those that nurture it.

At the helm of this are the Laws. The Law of Attraction, the Law of Reciprocity, of Abundance, of Manifestation. They are real and they govern our every move on a subtle level. What we give we get. The chrysalis knows this. The more time that it spends inside, the bigger and brighter it becomes. Resting within, knowing that the Universe has developed it in perfect form, in perfect timing.

It is the human mind that lacks patience for the Universe to bring what has already been designed specifically for you. It is the human mind that complicates the basics of life–being more, wanting more, extravagance, complexity. It is all very simple. It is within our nature to wander as humans, and yet we've created for ourselves a rigidity in thought, in place, and in time. We have bent into form the very concepts that were never meant to be molded and structured to be as they are. And so, we find ourselves in a box, unable to move freely and gracefully to where we are called to go.

The Knowing gives us these indications long before we become awakened. We fail to hear them and thus the alarm bells must ring louder and louder until it is hellbent that we listen. When we delay the inevitable is where discomfort joins us on our journey. Resistance to the Knowing is much like bending a spoon with your eyesight. It is only when you relax into and trust what is forming and occurring in front of you that you can truly believe and go with the flow.

There once was a prophet who said that "Those who flourish have waited for their seeds to be watered by the unforgiving and relentless unpredictability of the clouds. They form right in front of our eyes but whether they produce the result that we need can only be determined by a trust in the process." Assurance can never be provided, but in the process of patience lays faith and trust in the Universe to provide us with everything we need to serve it well.

Along the way we will find that trust builds. As the Universe sends us messages and events that can alleviate our sense of doubt, the trust in what we cannot see slowly grows. And when this builds to a degree that the questioning of ones' place within the Universe ceases, we begin to see more clearly. We lay down our guards, rest in the arms of the Universe and become one with the Knowing. Our hearts can release the walls that have protected it for lifetimes, the ego can drop its act, and we become what we are here to do. To spread our wings like a glorious monarch, exuding beauty and breathtaking grace wherever we go, and be a reminder to others of their potential for growth, transformation and beauty from a place of inner silence, strength, and peace within.

There comes a time when the resistance becomes too heavy to carry, straining when there is no need to. A divine timing for everything and everyone. There is no need to hustle or achieve. It is simply there for us when we are ready to spread our newly formed wings.

Chapter 6
Taking Flight

Our first flight with our new wings may be daunting but we've been here before, in previous lives and incarnations. That place of trying something great, never been done before, or simply just too big for our britches. But as we take that first step, leap, or jump we learn that we are capable. The questioning of our ability sets us back on our evolutionary journey, for we are capable and supported beyond measure and the doubt raises a wall against the Universe. That we do not trust what the Universe has made us into. Without exception the doubt will shape our misery to prove ourselves right. Like attracts like.

The Universe prefers to wait until that doubt cracks–that moment (or moments) in time when we question if this is all that is, if this is all we are made to be here on this earth. The response is a resounding "No."

In this moment, the Universe facilitates events to show us the way out of our limited belief system. A segue of sorts, a sneak peek into what is possible. A remembering of gifts, seeing into other dimensions, moments of premonition. From this point forward, taking flight has new meaning. You are seeing the world differently, of possibilities, of capacities that you were not able to see previously. When you are ready to take that flight now, there is a confidence, and assurance, that all will be okay. That you are carried gently by a team of helpers nudging you, leading you, picking you up if you fall.

The amazing gift that comes with being the butterfly is the joy in simply being the beauty that you are, being gazed upon, showing your colors, and fluttering joyfully through the trees and flowers. There is nothing to do but be beautiful. Be who you are, opening your wings to embrace each beautiful flight as an opportunity to go places and be with other forms of beauty on earth.

The flights that we speak of are our purpose to living. When we "take flight" we are living with purpose. Our flight becomes the pathway to evolution, each flight building upon the prior, growing stronger with each leap, attaining greater and greater altitudes as we endure the distance and challenges along the way. This stimulates an upward movement, ascension to new realms that we could not envisage or see previously until we achieved these new heights. These are not realms of power; rather, realms of the earthly plane that are experienced by those who have grown in confidence and awareness such that they can attain new layers of consciousness.

Moving between these realms is possible and common during the early ascension periods. A desire to stay with what is known while accepting the experiences and path that you are on. Breaking free from the lower realm attachment happens when you no longer see the value or benefit to yourself individually and to earth as a whole.

As you ascend, the darkness that prevails for significant periods of time allows you to be with who you are, wholly, unconditionally, in every aspect of your being. The dark corners are where we have abandoned ourselves, where pieces of us reside waiting to be seen, to be heard, by ourselves first and foremost. The remaining parts of us need to be brought back in order for us to be whole and inseparable for the rest of time.

The parts of us that have been exiled have much to teach us, about the separation that pains us when we didn't have the knowledge and understanding of the consequences of leaving ourselves behind in some place, relationship, or situation. There is a revealing of layers upon layers of guilt and shame that we harbor unknowingly when we leave ourselves behind. This can only be repaired by welcoming them back with open arms, willingly, softly, patiently; for to leave them behind again will cause breaks to the heart and soul that will keep us from our destinies.

Learning to receive back that which is us is the hardest part, for we had no prior knowing of the consequences. And so, we must deal with not only the awakening of our rejection of self but also the pain that this has caused to self and others along the way. It is no easy way through it but to dive in fully and completely.

Where there is a will to expand and see beyond ourselves, there can be forward momentum which is revealed as challenges of sorts. To test our determination and willingness to put in the work that will be required. This is not for the faint of heart. It is for ones who are ready. Others will eventually be ready too, but the pace cannot be changed by anyone other than ourselves.

We hold ourselves back when we are not ready to see, or when we are satisfied with the status quo. For some, sitting in this status quo will not be an option. Their destiny requires forward movement in order to be fulfilled and the nudges will be prominent in their life so that they cannot be ignored or avoided. Life will present opportunities to take, or it can throw you into the deep to make sure you learn how to swim towards your new life. **A life destined for greatness cannot be avoided. It can only be held back for as long as our purpose can remain on pause.** *The Pause,* however, does not last forever.

The pause can be seen and felt as an omnipresent standstill in time, where forward motion cannot be seen or felt, but arrangements are being made in the backdrop of your world. Coinciding with this pause is the pulling back of everything you are attached to, thus releasing the weight of your body and soul under your previous circumstances. These two events are coordinated in order to provide the best possible outcome and path for what could otherwise be a long and arduous process when surrounded by the daily activities of life as you know it.

The pause will detach anything that does not serve, anyone, or otherwise, that cannot be a supportive mechanism for your future. There are telltale signs—lethargy, lack of motivation for what previously gave pleasure, a standstill in projects that seemingly are going nowhere. These are all non-random events; they are purposeful and necessary to the overall process. Watch and see.

Harmonious interaction is what is key during this. Where a thought arises that reveals disharmony in a person, place, or thing, heed this as a warning to remove it gently for this period. It may not be forever, but this period is extremely sensitive to those things that are unaligned or incongruent with your immediate path.

Trust above all else that your body knows the way and will not lead you astray.

Trust in the divine path for it will reveal itself in due time.

Chapter 7
The Reckoning

Above all else in the heart of wisdom, is the presence of grandeur. This is not speaking of the power that Kings and Queens have established to portray their hierarchy over others. It is a grandeur of our own beingness and the grandeur of the world around us. It is all grand when we look at it through the heart.

Where once we saw just a limitless sphere of resources and material goods, we now see the connection of us all to the bigger picture, the purpose of our existence, the power that we hold–and have always held–that can lead us to destruction or to evolution. Take your pick.

We individually have the power to influence the whole. Our actions are recorded, the intentions reflected back to us when we do not choose in accordance with evolution. As the masses choose in this direction, the collective energy will be transmitting this and feeding upon itself. A downward spiral if we allowed it to. This is the purpose of individual awakening and the massive spiritual shift that is required to reset our evolutionary pathway.

From feeding our desires to hurting each other, these actions divide us from the heart-based actions we are meant to be taking on this planet during our evolutionary placement here. The path to awakening redirects us back to our hearts, the place of knowing, of love, of compassion so that we may choose differently. The heart of it all is for us to be an expression of our pure consciousness.

Residing in a place of division is not pure consciousness, it is evolutionary standstill. A prolonged suffering to those that have held ancestral trauma for generations, binding them and their progeny to ongoing suffering that permeates to others. A reconciliation between those of the current time and those of the past is needed to rebalance world karma and release suffering across the grid. Where one holds pain, others are surely sustaining the negative charge of that pain.

Holding on to our current ways is a matter of fear. Fear of the unknown. Fear of what liberation of the masses will cause when the current structures fall around them. What will create order, who will be accountable for the chaos? We all will be held accountable for reforming *a new way* and minimizing the destruction that freedom may temporarily create for those who do not yet see their role in the big picture. Harmless the rest will be, for they know the consequences of acting in a manner that perpetuates fear and chaos and the opportunity at hand. For there is no better place to create harmony from when the world has been turned on its head. When the demise of humanity relies upon each one of us working together, and the systems which kept us apart are no longer, we are ripe for change. Of the human kind.

Humanness. The kind that reveals itself during tragedies and fosters a working together. A banding, threading, and weaving to support each other. Events of the past–9/11, hurricanes, humanitarian events–are all based on the principle that where one succeeds we all succeed, therefore enabling others can ultimately serve our own and collective needs.

The concept of community has fallen by the wayside. Only in certain pockets of the world is true community being carried out. Where neighbors have each other's back, where there is not homelessness because our home is also the home of others. A simpler more unified approach to living and meeting our essential needs.

Gratitude. Satisfaction for living beyond the stuff we hold. A remnant of past civilization and tribes that were well organized and successful based on their collective beingness rather than their individuation.

Healing takes place when we are supported by others, trauma is less frequent when we are held closely by the hearts of others, wielding much greater and capable minds to choose for the good of all. This altruism is pure and intentional. It does not mean we do not fulfill our own desires, rather, the desires chosen are in support of the collective as much as they are for self.

This new place or era of being can only come when we drop our defenses and see ourselves and each other as we truly are. Genuine, humans, with hearts and souls that require nurturing and fostering, at each phase of our life.

We tend to see nurturing as only a phase during child-rearing, the mother and child relationship. But, it extends to all of us, at all times. Where there is not nurturing of the heart and soul, the fire fades, opportunities are dismissed, we begin to fall asleep. This nurturing is essential to bring upon ourselves and each other, and not cut off once we are at an age of independence.

Learning to nurture oneself comes from witnessing others who are kind and nurture themselves, who feed their body and soul with good things–whether foods, experiences or in communion with others. We observe others happiness and well-being and stimulate it for ourselves. Trying whatever comes our way, out of curiosity and intent to support our internal fire.

When was the last time you experienced joy?

When we ask this question of ourselves it is to remind us what we are here for. Not of self-gratifying experiences. Rather the joy that comes from igniting our fire *and* that of others. We all are here to serve each other. We often forget the "other" particularly when we are operating from a space of dullness and exhaustion. The kind of forced joy that comes when we feel we *should* be doing more. Rather than responding from a place of abundance for self and others we respond from a place of lack. Without sufficient resources to propel us into our natural state.

So where does one start when the kettle is dry? Leave the effort behind. **If there is efforting in order to bring joy, there is a force that is opposing what it is that is trying to be achieved.** Where there is flow–a lack of efforting–is where we want to be. Allowing for the joy to present itself in each moment. We do not need to create it because it already exists. We simply have not allowed it to come into physical form because we were rejecting it in some way. Through busyness, lack of harmony or patience, the many excuses for deferring that which will enable us to lead a great life. When we quiet ourselves we can see what we are resisting.

Wholeness is a process, a cycle of evolutionary proportions. It is what we seek and what is seeking us. To allow this cycle to happen within each of us enables planetary cycles to similarly function, with less efforting. The systems individually in harmony ultimately support harmony as a whole.

Chapter 8
Alivening

At the point in which we begin to see how easy we can make our lives, there becomes a lightness to our being and how we carry ourselves in the world. The weight that we once felt we needed to carry can be released for a new way. When we are living fully alive in all aspects, we do not carry or hold weight. We release all that is not ours to carry for a more conscious way of being.

Alivening can be seen as a stage of feeding our internal fire, stoking the embers, igniting our soul back to which it knows to be true. This is slightly different from awakening in that our intentions daily become a purpose unto itself. The intention of being alive in all manner of the word. Being here and now seeking positive experience for growth, allowing what is in the energetic realm to fuel us and feed our grandness.

This phase can be challenging for those who choose to dwell in the past, for the energies of the past will nullify any forward momentum that we are trying to build. **To be alive is to live here and now, not in the stories or drama that has already taken place.** There is no purpose that it serves to dwell there, only the perpetuating of the story.

To remain in forward motion requires a severing of all ties to the past, a releasing and clearing of the space and relationships that hold resentment or depict our less than whole state of being. To be fully released is to open your entire being to all the possibilities that are present, waiting to be realized. Harnessing the energies that are pointing backwards is the goal, to reverse their direction towards newness and vibrancy that is supportive of your wholeness rather than the fragmentation of where it came.

We often do not realize our attachments to the past–who we were, where we have been, what we have done–until we look at it clearly from the perspective of "what does it do for me now." If that past event has helped you learn and grow you are less likely to live there. If it continues to harbor emotions towards self or others, you still live there and have not learned what it is that the event required of you.

To learn is to also let go. Of the event, the story, the wrongdoing, to enable you to progress forward with a new way of seeing. All that once was is merely a representation of who we were back then, not who we are now. We have a tendency to attach to who we were in those points in time, that we were right in some way and others wrong. Yet we missed the whole lesson.

We are not required to sit in a lesson our whole life. We must apply the learning in our day-to-day, to see that applying lessons is not a matter of right or wrong; it is about the choices we make and the consequences that brought about our state of mind and being in that particular event. To learn and let go creates a more stable place of beingness that respects our need to grow (aka learn) and to continually live for more. To stop growing means we are not living for the true purpose of life here on earth.

Karma hampers this phase much of the time, for we are still working out contracts and dues in some way. These are not fully responsible for our suffering, but they play a part. Past life regression holds many keys to the underworld, our psyche, that has energetic attachments to prior lifetimes. These emotions are most often rooted in trauma and parts of ourselves that detached during those events. They can be brought back to self during the alivening process by opening portals to those lives and retrieving them and returning them back to our soul.

Soul retrieval has an important function in reminding us of our gifts, our longings, our premonitions of future states, and in making whole again our spiritual state of being. Our spiritual state and our physical state is so closely woven that our physical illness manifests from our soul that is seeking to be made whole. Our attunement to the needs of the soul will enable us to quickly return missing pieces and reframe our perspective on living going forward. Our new frame becomes that of the soul in its entirety and the purpose and destiny that it arrived here for, in the present lifetime.

Never underestimate the power of the soul in its unfragmented state. It has the ability to drive us to where we could never imagine going. To places, earthly and beyond, to experiences that support our aliveness, and to people that are meant to be with us on our soul journey. There are no mistakes, they are divinely orchestrated for the sole purpose of bringing us closer to magnificence, closer to wholeness.

Our destiny awaits.

The purpose of the intricate process of uncovering the layers to our destiny and the years of preparation that it takes is essential to the overall outcome. To *prepare* is to become ready. To be ready, in a state of acceptance.

Understanding of the nature of ourselves is necessary to be able to see even a glimpse of the grandeur that is possible within. Most of us will only seek to be great based on what it is we have seen within ourselves and the limits we allow the world to place on us. Grandeur is seen as unachievable, "out there" for others, not us. Even those who remotely touch the surface of grandeur do not believe in themselves as the reason for accomplishing it.

The preparing stage makes up most of the period we spend in awakening and alivening. Transiting through phases of growth all for the sole purpose of preparing our bodies at the physical, mental, and spiritual planes. For one to grasp the extent of preparation required is like asking to be foretold what it takes to become a neurophysicist. It cannot be described until you are in the thick of it, and even then, there is still yet more to see and live through.

When the time comes to experience this phase, you will feel vastness beyond comprehension. That you will never reach the "out there" that you long for because of intricacies in preparing for and the steps to get there. The vastness is not seen, rather it is felt, it is known to be there but intangible, indescribable, ineffable.

Just as the stars feel a million miles away, so does your destiny. In every phase of growth there are milestones–in exactly the manner of the word. Miles (distance), stones (pathway). The path of stones is carried on for miles so that you follow the markers at each stage, to become ready for the next leg of the adventure, or race, or journey. The stones are the bridge from here to there.

Tenacity in what we are willing to do is a matter of choice. That which you believe in will manifest to the extent in which you are willing to pursue its growth. The ineffable does not arrive to those who are unwilling. It shows up to those that are determined, committed, successful, and showing up for themselves day in and day out.

The experiences they endure is not for the faint of heart–which means also, that they are not easily fainting under the pressure while enduring such incessant expectations to be self-aware, self-reliant, remitting in strength and endurance. For the long haul, not just a period of one's life where you can then revert to prior times. It is a lifestyle, a life journey. It does not end until your soul releases from this incarnation and absorbs itself into new form, whether a new physical body or in guidance to those that are in process. The learnings here are of benefit not only to that particular soul but all those who touch upon it.

There comes a time when the ineffable becomes real. Tangible. When the physicality of what once previously existed only in energetic form comes to fruition. The aliveness that this generates is beyond words. It is the meeting of the future with the present.

What could only be felt becomes touchable, tangible, smellable. It is real. It has always been real, but only in the eyes who could see.

To see something come to fruition with their very own eyes is magical, brilliant. It releases all doubt in the abilities of our soul to extricate from desperate realities, a common, joint form that comes together for mutual need and belonging. A mutual determination to find one another, the missing piece to one's story. For where there is a missing piece in me there is an extra piece in you.

The marriage of souls recognizes to where they belong. They do not hide from one another. It is not possible. For the missing link creates, unbeknownst to the parties, a severing of souls that becomes unbearable, and a reuniting is bound to take place. The fusion of souls during the initial marriage is forever, across lifetimes, across time and space. There can be no other where there is a marriage of souls.[1]

Depicted in the art of Greek and gothic times is the invaluable connection between god and goddess, demarcated by the concept of white, of purity, of patience in thou beloved. For only he knows where they have been and where they shall go. Together they reach for each other's hand in an attempt to touch that which is so close but still beyond grasp. That which exudes the

---

1. We are attempting here to link the two seemingly benign concepts of marriage and awakening by bringing to light the separation of souls at a time of mutual deconstruction and reconstruction of each individual soul. Precarious as it may be, there is an order to the joint mission of two souls and they each in parallel must begin to see each other in the manner that they see themselves.

beauty of love, temperance, and joy without ever laying hands on one another. There is a knowing, a longing, a presence beyond anything imaginable. It circumvents all laws that govern the Universe, for it is the Universe within each other.

There is a mind-bending concept to consider when arriving to the place of awakening and alivening. Things are not as they are. You are not as you are. They are a mental construct based on years of prophesizing and explaining in scientific terms that which cannot be explained in the languages we have adopted.

Only the language of love can fully describe what is capable of our souls, of our infinite Universe and the biosphere that sustains life on our planet. Only a love beyond immeasurable proportions can execute such beauty and grandeur while withstanding the debauchery that is impregnated within the beings that reside on it. Only this love has the ability to forgive on a global scale for the purpose of its goal and intention of universal love. Where there is a willingness for retribution [give in return, restore] and forgiveness, there is a path towards grandeur.

Alivening can only be done within the confines of your individual psyche, and the conditions you place around it will either foster or forego the process. There must be clear and consistent presence, the goal of which is to center the body back within itself, become cognizant of the parts that have separated from the whole, and call them back into existence within the body. There is a quickening, a "catching up" phase that is created when all parts come together. A recovery of sorts to become reacquainted of the missing pieces of oneself and the memories that it holds.

These memories have always been there, but residing separately. Protected from the conditions that were not suitable for it to return to. It amasses to a reunion within, a celebration and a peacefulness when one can become whole again. The traumas we must acknowledge happened, but our soul never needs to be separate if we can ensure conditions do not support its fragmentation.

The coming together after trauma has occurred is central to surrounding a person in light and love that the soul can see, preventing its departure. There is much to be learned from the soul in what conditions it requires to be safe. From here, the physical body can create an environment that is protective, nurturing, and supportive of growth. From here, the spiritual body can expand safely into realms it requires to access in order to fulfill its spiritual purpose. From here, the Universe can speak to us individually and collectively to shift the path of the world and all who must collectively see its value for the infinite potential that it beholds itself to be.

There comes a time when ignoring where we are headed becomes detrimental to our beingness, when we fail to see the signs and take the path laid before us. There are cues, signals which must be followed, otherwise our destinies cannot unfold to their highest potential. Walking the path means listening and walking, listening, and walking. Never is there a more important time to do this than now. Our beingness is at stake, our connections to self are withering, and our loss of soul consciousness will never be repaired if we do not act now.

Chapter 9
The Making

Contributions in this world are always being made by those who see a need, respond to it, and do so with their heart intentions. There is a pride and passion that comes with leading from the heart and serving others. It fuels more, it fuels and drives others to do the same, to be and do better, the best, for themselves and for others. There is a progressive awakening, like dominos, when we can help lead the way for others. A like-mindedness arises, a community sense of partnership, a leveraging of each individual strength for the greater whole. This is the making of community that can sustain ourselves across all dimensions.

Community comes in different forms. Church being one of the foundations of collective belief, yet one must not be tied to the dogma of religion that is staged and led by those in some power position like a sermon of God. The collective community is best served when our power is equal. There is no sermon, but a sharing of gifts, knowledge, concepts for one another to accept as their own or to create new. Creating is the foundation of life–from birth to death–we are creating. One cell at a time. One thought at a time.

This is where all beliefs and systems come from. And how they are applied can create either a self-sustaining community or a self-sacrificing community. The difference being the intention, on an individual and collective level. One with the intention to impose their belief system onto others is malicious in that it takes power away from other individuals and the collective. The removal of powers from others disables the system—each part being essential to the whole. Reducing one's ability to make decisions based on their own soul contracts, destiny, and growth disables a whole section of the collective in which it interacts with. The web is intricately linked by our ability to maintain our own purpose, alignment with soul.

Watch what happens when you take a decision away from a person. Their energy crumbles, contracts, and withdraws. They are reduced. A concept that is not often equated to energy balance is reduction, and deficiencies created from the situations that either enable our beingness or disable it to purely physical form. This reduction is counter to what our humanity is intended to do. Evolution is founded on the principle of expansion not reduction. Therefore, creating a system or society which continuously reduces options, decisions, experiences, and individual growth will not be sustainable. We become robots, functioning purely from doing that which society has reduced us to.

It is fundamentally important to remain in a place of being to remain connected with our sense of expansion and connectedness to the greater whole, energetically feeding the expansion that we desire at our core. Limiting beliefs will further reduce our potential, acting upon ourselves in a way that does not reflect our true beingness. This brings us back to our need for being rather than doing. To remain connected with our true self and to the whole.

One cannot lead an expensive life when they are sitting in a reductionist environment. There is a constant energy that is battling internally. This is draining. This is burnout. When self cannot compete with the outer world. We often come to this place without realizing we have done so, a gradual, subtle progression of sorts. Until it's done. At that moment we can either say we want more to life or we continue down the mundane path.

We must first want and believe that we deserve more. We must first feel the despair and discomfort of being here, to be able to identify that an opposite to this must exist.

Everything exists with two sides of the coin. Where there is despair, there is contentment. Where there is self-pity, there can be confidence and gratitude. **Once we have established our ability to choose, we can begin *making* our life in a way that has acknowledged our sense of worth, our desires and capacity, and our willingness to be in the driver's seat.**

Fundamental to the making of our lives is the connection to soul. Otherwise, we are simply finding things to do to kill time. When we say kill time, it truly is a wasting of precious time on earth where we could be feeding our destiny and fulfilling our purpose. To be in the driver's seat means to be watchful, aware, listening, seeking each step that is for the highest good of your soul. The map becomes clearer, albeit only showing parts that you need to see in a particular map. We would lose the point if we saw it all.

The driver's seat is also a metaphor of being in control of one's destiny. We can either drive towards it or away from it. We choose. It is not destiny choosing, it is our ability to interpret the signposts and detours that either allow us to get closer or further away.

The signposts along the journey are meant to test your belief systems, your trust in self and the Universe, and that there is a bigger purpose. The journey, not the destination is most important, for you cannot reach your destination without one [the journey]. Taking a section of the map out will derail your learnings along the way and lead you to a completely different endpoint.

The making is also about creation of self, our beingness, who and how we want to be. From a matter of heart, this means kindness, compassion, patience, peace and fulfillment. The core values of being human. We often do not think of these as fundamental within our web of existence. Imagine a web that is loose and unsupportive, prickly. There would be a challenge in believing that environment could sustain us without some form of damage.

Selecting our way of being is capable of changing the environment around us. The people, situations, experiences. These can all shift our ability and substance from which we can create our world. Change the environment, the tools, and the people that help you or hinder you, can be all it takes to set in motion the things that you can create. A welder must be surrounded by the supplies, tools, and space in which to build, as does one whose spiritual mind is destined to create.

Listen closely to the environments which you are called to, the curiosities that fuel passion within you, and the people that foster your way of being. They are all leading you towards your very own making.

Chapter 10
Revelations

The "Art of Non-Doing" is to bring us to a place of contemplation, a silence, a void of sorts that allows us to completely sever the binds that we have to thoughts, beliefs, systems, cults, oppression, suppression, and all of the limitations that surround them. They all have unique ways to restrict our life rather than to open it.

Belief systems can be helpful in that they provide direction, a sense of belonging, and community. But what they do not provide is a connection to our higher consciousness and that of the Universe. There comes a time when the Universe has things to say, and they must come through.

Non-doing is an act born out of necessity and not desire. One does not implore to be lazy or stale in their day-to-day life. The being thrives on experiential activity. So why must we enter a period of isolation and non-doing so much so that we lose all interest in all things "outside" ourselves? It is of pure necessity to block out all that is not contributing to our connection with God, Source, and the Universe at large.

It is helpful to look at this phase in terms of growth on steroids. Sure, growth happens while you are "out there" in the world, but the most growth takes place when you are inside contemplation on a regular and frequent basis.

Lazy is not the correct word. An immense amount of energetic activity occurs during this phase that it can hardly be seen as doing nothing. There are changes occurring at the cellular level that require noise, anything unnecessary for that activity, to cease. To stop expending energy on anything that is irrelevant to that stage of internal growth and instead, revel in the knowing that your entire being will be repaired if you give it the time and nurturing that it deserves. A baby thrives under this nourishment, and you will too.

There is an immense factor of sensitivities that comes with this growth. You are no longer dulled to the energies that surround you like before. There is a certain amount of recalibrating that takes place to ease the disruption to the body systems and reduce the potential for catastrophic shock to the mind. The human mind has a tendency to bring negativity during a change, worry, self-medicating, and diagnosis. The medical system cannot respond to abrupt changes that are unexplainable. There is no use to go there for trivial pains that come and go with no apparent reason. These pains are taxing on the system, but recovery is possible through daily ritual and establishing safe space to allow these changes to occur.

You are not alone must be remembered. Alone is the concept of the mind–where we cannot associate our experience to anything common or tangible, and so we create in our minds a story that we are unique in this experience. But it is not. We are connected across the vast interconnected web of beings, and you will be supported by those that are in touch with your field of existence. Remember this at all times.

Choreographed, are the series of changes. Explicitly in order to stimulate the sequencing of your DNA that is preparing to come through. Our environment can signal a coming offline and online of genes that are expressed across our lifetime. This sequence is potentially the most important to ensure there are no further delays in our growth as humanity. This preparation by way of sitting with oneself in contemplation serves to quiet the mind and body, reduce its reactionary impulses at the nervous and cellular levels, and create a symbiosis of the functioning across systems in the body.

Dysregulation for a very long period wreaks havoc on the body and it takes time to rebuild a sense of harmonic functioning. Things such as removing irritants from diet and skincare, soothing the spirit, nourishment at the cellular and muscular level. Each of these provide a foundation for rebuilding, remembering, and recoding of our spiritual, mental, and physical being. The smallest of stressors will feel challenging and disrupt the symbiosis. How this is managed is a matter of practice, peacefulness, and commitment to self. There is no one or no thing that is more important than you in this period.

Surges in energy may result during periods of "on-lining"–DNA coming to the fore. These are meant to repair and resemble the growth spurts of childhood. Waves of aching pains, sleepiness, and then a surge of newfound energy. The system is being built as you function in your normal human world. "The system of systems" is here to manage your divine purpose now, that you have mastered the art of being a human being in physical form.

Simple steps can be taken to allow this system to online itself. Taking baths, sitting in meditation, lingering, recording, allowing. It all functions to serve you and cannot be avoided. To hinder it will create more pain due to the resistance that it creates. For now, your only activity is to allow what is needing to come through.

Allowance, the act of allowing [Medieval Latin: *allocare;* late 14c., from Old French: *allot*][1] is to enable space for something or all. All-being is the concept that we are within everything and everything is within us. We cannot restrict the *all* and therefore when we are in a state of allowance we are acknowledging and accepting all that is. There is a wider scope to the word than ourselves, and that when we allow into ourselves we are also allowing within all others.

To save space for healing and growing requires commitment. An ability to put aside those other life things that consume time and energy and devote time to opening our space to something bigger than ourselves. The revelations that come with this are profound. A connection to the bigger whole that we often know that it exists, but we can't place or give it form.

The bigger whole becomes us during this period by the access that we have to a source of energy and power that can make miracles

---

1. *to set aside for special purpose, to commend, praise, appreciate value of, take into account or give credit for, recognize, admit as valid*

happen. Within us and beyond us. This sobering revelation can make one completely detach from the world, knowing that they are so well supported on a universal scale that no physical system could humanly be able to comprehend it.

The purpose of our time here is expressed through generations and generations of experience at the physiological and cellular memory that is held within our DNA. Certain DNA codes lay dormant during periods that are not supportive of its expression. Laying in wait, these codes are imprinted with everything that your soul has endured, lifetimes of memories, experiences, transgressions that are needing to be seen and healed for the purpose of moving out of our *learning* existence and towards our *service* existence.

We have always had within us everything that we need to know to deliver on our purpose. When the time is ripe the cherry explodes. When we nurture the tree, fruit it will bear.

Coming to the point of revelations is no easy feat. It has already been a rollercoaster ride by this point and the notion of enduring even more can be hard to accept. In the acceptance is a change in how we experience this ride. It no longer becomes a rough and tumble road, rather it evens out, the corners a little less abrupt and the speed at which we see things come to fruition is increased. The long and arduous journey is more palpable, tolerable, and enjoyable. That, my darlings, is the revelation. Now let's enjoy the ride.

Chapter 11
Intentionally Blank

Intentionally left blank.

Chapter 12
Elevating One's Purpose

There can be only one type of dharma. One that is connected to the heavens and the earth below. Other types of dharma exist but it is for the purpose of soul mission and not for collective mission. The collective mission is one of divine potential that allows the earth to balance the scales of polarities and consequences.

There once was a saying that "the two eyes must see before they can understand the truth of themselves and the world that exists to serve a greater potential than ourselves." To see, to truly see, is to perceive one's being down to the core of self. To the basics of survival and in expression of the higher power of being, there are great powers that require mastery.

From seeing within to then seeing without, there must be a dedication to one's dharma that is resolute, unwavering, unrelenting towards the influences of the external world. There is only one true mission when the world depends on it for survival.

Survival of the fittest is regarded as the most basic evolutionary principles. It was never meant to be exclusive of all beings and creatures, rather, a stepping stone to the greater world above. To survive the fittest means you have the power to outrun others. But the world above requires not physical power and capacity, but a capacity to go beyond what is known to others, accessing levels of consciousness that are known and unknown.

Access to these worlds are not for the few and far between, they are for all who choose to go there. If only one can perceive this great power–beyond fitness. It can only be seen through the eyes of those who have endured the awakening, alivening, and remembering stages. To be *seeing* is to know what exists beyond the imaginable, trusting the powers of one's own heart, and turning that trust into the power of creating.

Creating one's own destiny can take many forms. While destiny is the final outcome, truly creating is one's path towards that destiny. Taking turns for the purpose of heart-based fulfillment can be prime for accelerating one's path towards destiny. A facilitation, priming a tangible step or steps, leaping, laddering, or extending oneself to other places that access the divine potential. Taking these steps can be extraordinary in meaningfully engaging oneself with their environment, their trueness, to connecting their innermost desires.

There is no wrong decision when it is taken from this space.

There is no wrong route to destiny when it is made with thought and intention to crafting a world of greatness and grandeur for self and others.

Heavenly guidance will steer away from steps that are not forward moving. But there can be a purpose to this also, when other variables are needed to align on one's path. Extreme actions may be required to reroute if the path is too far from one's dharma. Opportunity will always be created for those who are challenged by understanding or sensing these deviations from the soul. Allowing these interventions to take place is Gods way of redirection, of guidance and support, never a form of retribution or punishment. It is when we do not listen to our internal compass that we need this guidance the most.

Taking one's dharma seriously is a necessary step before access to higher consciousness can be allowed. Manipulation of access to wisdom for purposes of greed or power can cause severe havoc to one's health or their journey to the divine. Irreparable in this life because what was required to be learned has not been sufficiently applied. To learn is to understand *and* to apply.

Situations that test our ability to apply are frequently provided in order to practice, to experience, and enable endurance on one's path. It is not a skill that can be established through one experience. A multitude of demanding and enabling processes are being applied with each attempt at moving towards one's destiny. Often subtle and embedded within our subconscious, they test each moment of our day in which we are either progressing or regressing. This is neither bad nor good but establishes a type of check-in system that is connected to our higher power.

To be receptive to this guidance is key and helps in learning what is meant to be for ourselves and related to our purpose, and not. To be held up in a frivolous state of being has no purpose to the greater whole of humanity and mankind. To be here, in the moment, and with purpose, allows for evolution to take place.

Challenge yourself every day to connect to your dharma, purpose, wholly and fully to see the essence in you change. From just being, to living that truth which rests inside of you. Hold this throughout your day and activities, whether they are related to dharma or not, for the essence will permeate and create new opportunities for you to instill your worth and creation within everything that you do. To be wholly imbued within your truth, essence, dharma, is to live as you were intended. This intention holds greatest power above all effort that is needed to proceed in life.

You are here to live in this way. Without effort. With intention only.

Holding yourself close during this elevation period allows distractions to fade away, move around you, so as not to take you off course. They will have less and less affect over you over time. You may feel alone or introverted, but this is necessary for all else to fall away. That which is not connected to your purpose will slowly but surely find a way out of your day-to-day life. Whether job, relationship, or extra-curricular activity, they will not hold. There is no longer a place for them to attach to.

Your pure intention cannot be messed with. In the end, this pureness is what allows you to move through life with ease and joy. This, is pure being.

Will you take the call to higher living if it means ease and joy, despite the shedding that must take place to get there?

Will you let go of things when they no longer serve your higher power and goal as a human?

These are fundamental questions that one must ask before embarking on the journey in order to move through it with most ease and grace and with least hardship. If all would be gone, would you be okay so long as you were in your truth? This is not insurmountable but is where many get caught up in the current materiality of being. Your worth surely is more than that which exists in material form. How else are you to find yourself when these items choke and cease your energy, leaving nothing for your spirit to hold?

Chapter 13
Embarking on the New Path

Challenges will arise due to the blocks within the body systems when they have not cleared sufficient density. There is a grit to it, a stickiness that can be unbearable at times if one does not care sufficiently for the body. There are many practices that can lead to a more fulfilling path because there are less obstacles and bumps in the road while dealing with fundamental changes to the body systems.

Weakness in the body core can wreak havoc on the internal organs as they try to move and shift back to their neutral position. The liver can be a big factor in making healthful changes as it houses the life force of the vital organs and can become clogged due to everyday stressors and contaminants. Bile from the kidneys is essential to be flowing, preventing a buildup or accumulation of minerals in excess of what is required at any one point in time.

To stimulate bile production, eat leafy green vegetables daily and incorporate warming foods at night. Warming foods include soups and stews, fewer cold salads at dinner time, and equal portions of carbs to proteins. Excess bile will be a marker of efficient detoxing and purification and can be smelled within the urine as a pungency at nighttime. Even though extra bile may not be needed on a daily basis, it will assist to regulate the endocrine system and level of hormone production.

Hormones produced during this stage of evolution is primarily for the purposes of pituitary gland stabilization. The intense production during the awakening stage when the pituitary gland is at its peak intensity is alleviated by foods that are cooling to the system, much like a temperature regulator. But this is important to be done in the early part of the day so as not to affect bile production at night.

The first thing that should be consumed is a glass of cold water. Contrary to current belief about the benefits of warm lemon water first thing, there is an important factor missing from the equation. The digestive system, when functioning properly, needs no stimulation. It regulates based on periods of fasting versus consumption. At any point in time, warming foods may overstimulate the endocrine system to the point of excess heat resulting in a breakdown of tissues lining the epithelial cells of the stomach, which correspond in memory of all other cells related to it. This means the stomach lining is interconnected to the skin barrier at the place of consumption. These patterns are etched within memory at the cellular level and can be changed with proper repatterning. Cold foods first thing in the morning will invigorate cells without overheating, blood flow is stimulated as vessels contract–as with all cold therapies–vasodilation occurs as a healing mechanism rather than a coping mechanism.

Extraneous materials build up in the digestion system because of a lack in simple habits for healthy living. Fasting provides a rest for many bodily functions while cells are able to focus their function on growth and renewal. Key to this process is mitochondria, which act as energy gatekeepers to many functions in the body. Mitochondria require continuous exchange of growth hormone, and when the body is tied up in processes, growth hormone is diverted away from its primary function. Rest of the nervous system is foundational to providing ample time for this process. Muscle repair after frequent or continuous intense exercise will deplete growth hormone that is necessary for cellular rejuvenation and energy release. One must reconsider the purpose and function of their activities on a day-to-day basis and remain in balance of level of physical activity and restful activities.

Restful activities do not deplete, rather they bring homeostasis to the body. Yoga, Pilates, meandering type of walking, bring a specific tranquility to the body despite the amount of efforting involved. It is the mind's way of seeking balance while allowing for active movement that is not deteriorating itself. There can be some invigorating exercise during the course of the day when the body indicates it to be appropriate.

Well-being in this phase is paramount. The body adapts best in times of stress when the base level of well-being is at its highest. This should be the goal from this point forward and include various modes of generating body and mind satisfaction, calmness, and peacefulness such that any additional stress is a mere blip in the radar rather than a long and drawn-out phase. Inhabiting your body in every moment brings an attunement that will help to measure a stressor against. Extreme sensitivity will arise when an undue stress cannot be avoided. The sensitivity will diminish the sooner one can bring themselves back to homeostasis.

The world was not meant to be this extreme in attunement but the process of remembering is such that it requires attention to detail and an expanded sight in order to bring all relevant information to the foreground. It is this information that can stimulate us poorly and necessitate measures to bring back the self into the foreground.

Harmony in the self is paramount at all times, for the Universe is aligning itself based on the positioning of you in the centermost point. Random deviation may not result in a different affect unless it is far from alignment with soul. A misaligned position will create negative energy sources, thus extending you in the wrong direction. Keeping soul aligned enables various aspects of future possibilities to reorient themselves in the best manner. A misalignment will feel heavy, hurt or cause great discomfort in one or more bodily systems. They function in harmony with the clear alignment of soul to Universe, magnetizing all other aspects of your purpose and Akash.

The reason you are here will be revealed when you are in pure alignment with all that is to be learned for the sake of your fulfilment in this lifetime. Pure harmony can be felt and seen, for the magic exudes through the aura when one is at their highest potential.

Chapter 14
Remnants of the Past

Our memories of the past overtake our ability to live in the present moment. From lives passing by to literal lives of the past, we are meandering always between the things that once were and the things that are in the here and now. Time deceives us, for we can feel what once was and reach into the future and touch what will be. There is no difference. Time is one. We are one with time. The lapses between space is what we feel as separation between then and now, a metaphorical distance to be clear. For there is none. Only here. Only now.

Can you imagine a place where it all happens as one? Then, now, here, there?

Our minds are endless in the places that we can be, yet in the construct of time, one moment must end before the next can begin. This is absurd. There can be only one place.

We look back upon history to understand where we have come from, yet we cannot bear to look within ourselves for those same answers. They are all within us. We have each lived through the histories of our past, we have endured, we hold the experiences equally as our ancestors did. They are within us at all times. We hold their memories and their wisdom resides deep within each of us. Why won't we go there? We read novels upon novels, historical records and storytelling from those that are still here to tell about it. Yet we will not listen to our own inherent wisdom. We cannot bear to see ourselves as naked and raw as our bodies have been, watching our soul endure reckless life after life. We cannot face the truth that we have forgotten over and over again, not being brave enough to stop and breathe our own fire back into ourselves.

Where can we begin to look at ourselves as our whole experience; from beginning to end?

Where can we accept that what once was has the opportunity to change, to be better, more loving, kind and compassionate? To ourselves and to others. Right the wrongs of our past and begin anew.

Why can we not give ourselves the grace of a new life, a new way?

Instead, we linger in the memories of the past, bound to stay there forever if we allow ourselves. There must be a different way, there must be an exploration why we hold ourselves in this pattern. We can break free, but we choose not to.

What a wonder it is when the shackles of daily living break away, enabling our day-to-day flow to occur on its own accord, as we need, what we need, by way of instinct, intention, and intuition. They, are the three "I"s of life. Not the two eyes that we see through, but the three integral body ways of knowing and doing. They, are inherent. The physical sight is only there because of our physical nature.

The three "I"s are present for the soul, to lead, to seek, to know where it is best placed, from one moment to the next. There can only be one way of seeing once you awaken and remember. Vision is no longer a physical sense, it is a greater ability. An ability to see beyond space and time, to observe, reflect, feel and exude the way forward. Here, there is only one way. Clear direction, cohesion across physical and spirit self, and cohesion across all selves. All come together as one again. All experiences make up the whole that we are here in, today. And thou shall continue to be whole.

Where there is a willingness to collapse all lifetimes and experiences into ourselves, we may see with great clarity the purpose that we hold and the service that is meant to be provided. Here, is the key to sustaining our evolution, our growth, our majestic being. When we let everything go to be as it is there is a freedom to *be*. There are no more memories, no more psychic spells. No more confusion about where we exist from moment to moment. They all are. They just are as they are. Deep acceptance. Deep knowing. Nothing can change what is. And so it is.

The familiarity we have with the past lands us to living there rather than being here. We succumb to the fear of the unknown, we strive to control, to know, to direct the course of events. But of course, we cannot. We can only flow with what is, how it is, and when it is. This is life. This is living. This is what was decided by you and me when we embarked on this human journey. We agreed to keep learning, choosing, doing until we could no longer bear the thought of not being who we are in our truest form. Spirit. Soul. Source.

We are one and there is no denying that which is inherently within us. Our lives must be a lie then, we say. No, our lives were meant to help us return home. We chose how long it would take and what barriers we would put in the way. We can also choose then, to remove those barriers and return home when we choose. It is "now or never" they say. Or is it?

Technically, there is a way to balance the present and the past. With our knowledge of the past we can make better choices, better ways of being and doing, less control over the outcome, knowing all will be well. A trust coming from our inner knowing that what is meant to be will come in divine timing and will be better than what we expect it to be. Out past limits us to seeing things in a better way.

What sets us apart when we allow the past to inform and not control our daily lives is that it continues our flow as beings toward the divine. It resembles a watercourse, multiple routes and boulders to navigate, but we always make it to the ocean where we belong. We will. Always. Whether we erode the boulder over time because we resisted going around it is a form of control. Not allowing things to be as they are. Moving is a motion that can hinder or help us depending on how attached we are to the meaning of the motion. If it defines us, we will experience hardship from the perspective that one cannot attach to anything because it is neither here nor there. We can only allow if we are to get anywhere.

The whole purpose to our experience is to allow for things as they are. When we are children, we knowingly do not control because to do so is futile. The greatness of the Universe, the speck that we are. Despite being a speck however, we are not powerless. We have magic to unearth, not control. Children can do this spontaneously in how they live their day to day lives. Being and doing. Being and doing. Without restraint on the playground, in the forest, in the water, they are able to feel the magic that surrounds them. When we remove those freestyle living approaches and build a structure around them, we take away the opportunity to flow in a manner that their body truly wishes. It constrains them, whether we intend to or not.

We capitalize on this by justifying the long-term purpose of learning and doing to prepare for adulthood. But, the human body knows not in how we as society have chosen to define adulthood by competency and class. Rather, it tends towards building capacity through intuitive knowing, feeling the surroundings, knowing what is meant to be in their life and not, choosing based on their spiritual guidance which we no longer give opportunity to speak for "the parents know best" concept. We don't know best. We only know *our* way, which is not the only and certainly not the best.

Navigating a childhood that allows for freedom of spirit and recognition of individual truth is simple. Live and let live. The pure meaning of this is that through life we learn how to live, and through allowing to live we live far greater than the eye can see. If we each aspired to do this form of living, we would not be caged by our lifestyles, our career choices, our limited aspirations, and failure to see our grandeur. It is quite simple really. **Flow where the water wants to take you.**

Chapter 15
The End of the Line

When we awaken, we begin to see ourselves for who we are and where we ought to be going. We give ourselves permission to become the water in its purest sense. Fluid, mobile, flexible, knowing. We become what we were born from. The waters of the womb have taught us since formation that we can trust, we can see both within ourselves and outside ourselves by the simple concept of energetic transference. What mother feels, I feel. What I feel, mother feels. Such a simple concept that we fail to give credit and consideration to the power of the human body.

Illuminated we become when we create from this space of knowing and peace with all that is. There is no disturbance, no waves, no contention. There lives within us this stillness, ambience of true, pure transcendence, yet so few of us get there.

For when we truly see, we thrive. We embark on a journey of trust, of faith, in ourselves and our world.

We combat the feelings of otherness by being intimately connected with the other world through our hearts and thus there can be no challenge unknown when the heart knows what is in its best interest. There is no challenge because what is presented is meant for, not against, our betterment. It is not a failure to succeed less than what we desire; it is succeeding in a range or gradient of ability based on where we reside on our path.

The challenges we experience in the earthly realm are part of our existence, perfecting this complex orchestrated world of opposites. For every given action there is an equal reaction, its orientation towards positivity is based solely on the energetic nature that has created it. And so, it returns in the same manner, shape and form. To be expecting anything different is not based on the laws that govern us.

There must be a frame in which this game is played, not rules per se, but principals to guide our presence here. It is a source of evolution that has not and will not leave us, rather it forms space for us to continually measure our progress over time. Are we still living true to those principals despite of or because of our progress over time? If we are not, how can this reality become pure of potential? This is the meaning of the laws. To create an ongoing source of potential and a mirror to see our existence within.

Take for example the mere act of being. This pure potential resulted from an inexplicably complex systems of cells, biology, repair and renew, automatic versus autonomic functions, living purely for the sake of unearthing our greatness. We already were great, so how can we become magnificent? These little (and not so little) advancements in our history have expanded our knowledge of how things work, but have also contracted them by the singular fact that we exclude the spiritual system from our sphere. We cannot comprehend it, so we ignore it.

But what if it is the centermost point of our existence? We then have failed to see the most important part of ourselves, and our potential will become more and more limited over time. We will have seen all that there is to see with our physical eyes and mind and growth will stunt. There is no more room in the box that we created for ourselves. Only a cramped life where we fail to thrive.

The notion that we are One gives us a faint glimpse at how much further we can go, but still, it is self-limiting. What then of us if we truly are a single piece of fabric interwoven? What does that truly give us beyond a recognition that our actions affect someone or something miles away? It merely creates a new paradigm for which we will become constrained in for the next coming century.

It is far bigger, greater, than we can possibly imagine. There are sensing capabilities not yet within our grasp that can have profound effect on how we live our daily lives, to suit our betterment of humanity as a whole and to regulate the effects of prior generations. Intergenerational effects cannot be dismissed, they cannot be relegated to only the most serous cases of trauma as the Holocaust. There are severe repercussions from the day-to-day decisions our ancestors made on our very ability to live coherently in this generation.

The familial lines are structured such that the presence of cords do not break, they amplify. The effects are not mere traits and patterns, but full-blown belief systems that are being carried forward into future generations that do not want nor deserve to live out our consequences. They deserve a pure chance, as pure beings with unlimited potential, not constrained by our current livelihoods and fateful experiences. When we can break these cords within us, we can minimize the continuation of failed attempts at humanity as spiritual beings. **To step forward as spiritual beings necessitates the resolution of all that binds us to the past. Energetically, this is paramount. Spiritually, this is non-negotiable.**

It is said that the ties that bind are inherently ours. This it true. Inherent. Inherited. Taking the spiritual lens to this means our innate ability to transfer energetic ties from one period to another has the capacity to limit us from future growth. Binded we are when we are tied–knowingly or unknowingly–to the past that was never ours to hold onto. The seers and the sages have seen this all along, but few have been able to convince the masses of the destruction that it can cause when we fail to acknowledge our internal power to heal from these bondages.

Cords are placed where they are at the time of the experience. They flow energy between people, even things, to create the energetic exchange and the opportunity to reconcile past belief systems through unconscious communication. But, when our attempts to reconcile are thwarted by the inability to energetically and spiritually communicate in a "clean manner" is that nothing gets reconciled. It cannot pass through as it was intended. Clogged, dirty, foreign.

Transmitting through cords allows for the exchange or rebalancing of one's energy and the history that reside between those individuals. If done purely and with intention to return to balance, it will reset the cords to their original state and detach where there is no longer an energetic or spiritual place for the connection. Where there is further work to be done as individuals jointly for mission purposes, the connection will remain open, enabling divine instruction to pass through.

Normally, there is a sequence to energetic cording that contributes to divine purpose. Purging, releasing, purifying, reclaiming, and reconnecting. These steps are necessary to fully re-establish the pure divine connection and purpose between individuals, their seeing capabilities, and other receptors that are activated upon divine instruction. The release of past traumas further opens the door to more meaningful understanding of one's own purpose and of those in their lives. One family, one source, many embodiments.

To own or be in one's own body is a misnomer. There have been many bodies before you and there will be many more, that carry your energetic signature. Across family lines, generations and generations go by where your cellular fabric is interwoven across others. Here, there is the ability for cellular DNA to become wound up in the past, particularly where energetic ties keep them wrapped within cycles. These cycles prevent us from moving past certain limitations of being. To sever these cycles is to no longer energize the past, to break free of the ties, and establish new ways of doing and being. To generate new possibilities, forms of thought and expand our minds outside of the energetic chaos that has built over time. The space in-between is needed for there to be a transition from old to new.

The new has a way of coming around. It passes by us unknowingly because we are too distracted in daily living that we miss the signs, the opportunities to do things differently. We are inherently inclined towards the status quo when there is no obvious reason or bigger picture to change. To change our way for the better requires us to feel into the way things were versus how they *could* feel.

The option A or option B test applied to our intuitive knowing can be a remarkable way to become more aligned to the bigger picture. The bigger picture holds an energy that will compel you over others. It will make itself known. It will reappear over and over again as long as required in order to be seen, to be heard, and to be acknowledged.

In finding that resonance, we find the solution. We find the bridge that will allow for our own divinities to pass through us, to challenge our historical truths, and to acknowledge where one must go. This applies equally to the collective consciousness, where group solutions can be found when the rhetoric is dropped and the space made for change, for new ideas, new ways of being that enable each individual to flourish.

What would happen if you challenged the status quo?

What would happen if you dealt with the bad apples as individuals rather than assign them all with the letter V? There would be much more resiliency, more ownership of the choices each individual made, and an accountability to that choice.

Where does the balance lay in societal function versus individual choice for the purpose of prospering within that society?

We must find the balance for the sake of coming into our own truths, our own purposes, and our soul's contribution to the whole. If not now, when?

If we get to the end of the line and do not challenge the status quo, we continue the cycle that binds us.

Chapter 16
The Ways of Old

Contemplating the status quo and how we got here requires a thorough understanding of energetic relativity, the construct under which the human race was created. Not to be confused with the theory of relativity.

There is in motion everything that lay before us and that which is ahead of us not yet realized. There is not one action or inaction that is unaccounted for in the grand scheme of Universal Law. It eludes us because we cannot grasp the concept of the future being already here and now, only for us to make a sudden shift in our course of being that diverts us away from what is destined. Allow. Allow things to take place. Make no decisions. There are not any to make. When we let go of the grip that we have on the notion of choosing our own destiny, by the simple fact that we cannot choose it, is an oxymoron. You cannot choose something that is already decided and the thought that you do is merely an attempt to control.

Control is at the root of historical trauma, in *ALL* cases. There is a need that is rooted in a belief system of power over others and ourselves, which leads to controlling behaviors and actions. Control is driven primarily by the fear of the unknown. The unknown being the greater force that dictates our destiny. We do not believe in the benevolence of this force, and so we try relentlessly to control how it plays on our psyche, our environment, our structures. To have no structure at all creates a fear of chaos, yet it is here, in the absence of structure that our freedom lays. To do as we feel, as we wish, from one moment to another.

Destiny does not care of our level of educational attainment or achievements in the world. It only concerns itself with enlightenment. Have you learned from your ways and see God through the eyes of your soul. Each moment is an opportunity to come back to this simple principle of seeing ourselves wholly such that we can see more clearly beyond ourselves to the true nature of Source/God.

What would we see if we looked from the eyes of the soul you asked? Pure love. Pure light. No body to inhabit, nothing beyond being. What you are, each and every moment.

There is a trust that is required to go here, to let go of all that defines us, flesh, bone, skin, thoughts, organs, systems, physical senses, beliefs, knowledge. Everything that we think makes us actually has no relevancy at the end of it all. And here is where we must dive straight into the purpose of this book. It just does not matter. We live the course of our lives, to be and to experience. **We bring nothing with us except for the goodness that we have created for ourselves, our family, and our society as a whole. Goodness is at the center of being. To be anything else is not**

acting from light. This is our biggest lesson which we have not learned.

When we impose judgement on others–is this acting from goodness?

When we take more than we need–is this goodness?

When we seek power over others or of a situation–is this goodness?

Of course, goodness is always in the eye of the beholder, and here is where history has made its mark.

From time immemorial we have sought to gain. Things, places, land, objects, people. This gain fuels our need for more, not only as compared to ourselves but also of others. This lack mentality, of seeking always more than what exists in front of us–knowledge, physical items–is at the core of all wars and power struggles, familial feuds, and economies that fall away. There is a constant need to keep up and a fear of not being enough. We have set the bar over the course of history, we cannot bear to not succeed, and so we pit ourselves against each other in order to win the race.

What race is this exactly? The race to extinction is exactly where we are headed at the pace of our current need for power and control. Greed breeds more greed. Power feeds the greed, ever so fuelling and simmering in the background. We refuse to let go.

Bear in mind that the advancements we have achieved are noteworthy. Medicine, science, technology. But to what end if it is not for goodness? We can all argue that many of these accomplishments were born from a "good" notion; but in the end, is there goodness for all of humanity? Or, is it setting the stage for the rich and powerful under the guise of goodness? There are always people who fall as a consequence of modern advancement. And taking the fall for the goodness of others is contrary to our own soul's needs. We are not meant to take the fall for others when their own desires fuel incoherency with their own soul's purpose of goodness.

So where does this leave us, when we cannot advance in the absence of affect on someone or something?

We must at this juncture, let go and allow destiny to take its course. Remove your hands from the reigns and pause. Pause until the wheels are in motion in whatever direction it is meant to go. Take your foot off the gas until guided to put it back. You will be guided if it is your destiny.

To continue on with no regard for destiny is like choosing poor quality food when your body needs nourishment. To treat your vehicle (your body) as anything other than pure goodness is divesting yourself from the greatness that you are meant to be. This is not speaking of accomplishments, it is in terms of our own heart-led ways of being that have a positive impact on others and their return to their light. Simple and powerful but dismissed at most times. Our collective consciousness is set in their ways and needs to come home.

Even when there is clear guidance provided to you to begin moving again, you do so in concert *with* your guidance not without it. It *needs* you to conspire with it in order to make the most of its plans for you. With you, it is co-creating, but in the absence of your acceptance of its plan it will be much harder for you to follow that plan.

Take for example, a crow that has diverted from its flock based on guidance. It was comfortable to stay with the flock–known, safe–but he chose to listen. He was in this very moment opening himself to all possibilities and aligning with the highest by letting go of the need to be safe and surrounded by his fellow flock. Now sure, something bad *could* happen, but there are many more possibilities of good and great than there are bad. We tend, as humans, to focus on the bad, as if that is the highest likelihood. It is truly not. In the realm of possibilities, there is more chance of good and great. Likewise, he opened up to new ways of thinking, to be welcoming of ideas and concepts outside the norm.

The norm hides us. It prevails because it is easy, justifiable, reassuring. Compounding that, is the sense of unease which we typically only ever associate with negative outcomes rather than the excitement that it may be trying to form within our existence, something good if not better than before.

Serious thought needs to be given to how we hold ourselves back from growth, experience, and change. **When we limit our own potential, we also limit the collective, our future generations.** In harmony, we become when we listen to our deeper, more innate calling as this is tied to our purpose and unification of all beings.

Gone are the days of survival of the fittest. It is no longer relevant or required if our goodness holds us all together. This is not to say we will never die or experience anything negative, it is merely the notion that it is not a result of the negative intention of others–conscious or unconscious. It is free of the ties that held us in those states, it is limitless and chooses for the better of all. Not as a martyr or a saint, but in pure goodness. When there is a pure goodness only more goodness can become of it.

Ordinarily, we think of old ways of doing things as the better or more wise choice because it was rooted in more than just our material ways of the current time. But they were equally as fraught with negative intention. Self-serving, growth of one more than another; perceptions of power that are often built on the concept of hierarchy and entitlement over another.

The root of change is here. That we are all the same, as equals, in deserving of all that the Universe has to offer. When we are willing to break the ties with the constructs of the past. They are called constructs for a reason. We have made them, therefore we can also see that they come to pass. For the goodness of our planet, our humanity, and all that is.

Chapter 17
Where Have We Gone

Where do we go when we detach from our bodies, unable to remain in a place so utterly devoid of meaningful attention and oblivious to our true nature? When we detach, we break apart, in parts. We reside in different places or experiences based on their importance–good or bad–to our soul. They either satisfy and ease our need because they are in some way more aligned than where we are currently, or, a piece is stuck in that place, jarred (literally) and unable to move back to self due to trauma. It remains there until we welcome them back.

The problem is, we often do not know that they are gone until our detachment wreaks havoc on our bodily system. To be pulled apart is akin to having missing toes–they each provide balance to the body, transfer weight equally, such that our steps and motions can be smooth, transitional, and with relative ease. Take any one of those away and you have instability. Foundational to our wholeness is for all pieces to be intact. Whole.

Fragmentation is another word often used for this brokenness. The mirror shattered, we do not see clearly. We do not even see that we are, the glaze giving the impression that all is well and that we simply need to chalk it up with strength, more power, more exertion. We are going the wrong way when we do.

To recognize these parts, being willing to witness their departure, each and every one, is necessary from a place of vulnerability not power. Acceptance and release of the story that led to their departure. It does not matter in the end, it happened. All that is required of us is to accept them back with open arms, gratitude, and compassion. For they are the beginning to our end. They must be present within us to complete us, otherwise we are not whole.

Brokenness should not be construed as a negative state or place. One is not damaged beyond repair. It is simply functioning as it was intended to. Bringing our awareness to it is not a failure but an imperative step to fully realize our existence. That in accepting an event which has taken place, we must have fully felt the course of emotion driven by the energy of it all, and to have let it go. Each and every time. Avoidance breaks. Holding breaks. Judgement breaks. It all must pass through for us to remain intact. We have not learned sufficiently from prior generations how to do this.

Certain people are able to transform this energy more easily so as not to build up or retain in the system. Sages of the past have always said "Be like water. Flow. Flow with the current, not against it." But we have trouble doing so. Our minds relentlessly in control of our every thought, motion, even before there is a need to respond or react. We have already thought of and live the consequences when we worry or think our way through an inkling of something happening to us. We devise a plan of events and then wonder why they have happened to us. They are merely thoughts taking form.

All actions have a prior thought that is driving it. Whether we like it or not, there is a cause to every action and a reaction to every cause. One which we should think about more carefully, before we make or take the actions we do.

For any moment that passes, there have been multiple other moments that could have enabled us to change our course. When we are not aware of them, they fail to take form. There lacks an energy to move it to fruition. This is the importance of being aware, of all that is or is not in our plane of sight. Just because we cannot see it does not mean that it does not exist.

Similarly, just because we see it, also does not mean it exists. We see that which we want to see. To feel, however, goes beyond the five senses that we so heavily hedge our bets on. When you *feel* the correct course of action, there will be no other that can be taken. It has an element of already *being* to it that cannot be denied. That is because it is. It exists, maybe that it is in a future time or place, but it *is*. There is no refuting what can be felt so deep within our bones. It is there, we are simply not aware enough to allow it to unfold naturally and without our every control in the matter. With ease it comes when our hands are off the wheel.

Driving requires sight, yes. But navigating the fields of possibility are a different story. Possibilities are endless, but the ones that are meant for you find you. An attraction to each other you are, because there is a fundamental gravity to you. As the earth's gravity holds the moon and the atmosphere in place, so does our hearts and everything that is a match to it.

The heart's resonance can be thought of as a gravitational pull. Resonance, meaning that which corresponds to the highest level of frequency towards that which belongs. There is no getting it wrong as we stand in that field of possibilities. There is no wrong ones, but the right ones made for you will find you. Let go of the wheel my dear ones.

A little lie may seem to have no consequence, but what if that one lie were to shift your aura? Shift it in such a way that the possibility made for you could not find you?

Your aura represents your frequency at any point in time. It responds to your every move, day or night. It releases excess energy while sleeping, creating space for clear and pure energy to form again. This is why sleep is so crucial to the awakening process, to allow your subconscious to purge through your dreams and resting periods. Not all sleep is created equal. Anything that jump-starts your heart will generate too much energy for the body to hold onto, disrupting the balance that sleep is trying to gain. Your aura will need careful attention so as to minimize disruption.

Restorative sleep can be gained when the mind and body have been given ample time to "download" or process the thoughts of one's day and to release them before sleep. Meditation enables both a release of thought and a slow decline in respiration and activity in the body. Being mindful that not all meditation is created for the same benefits, avoid guided meditations before bed as they require attention towards the guide rather than one's own body.

Stimulating the aura for best positive productive states can be done when showering, amplifying the stimulation to the scalp. Many neurons exist there which can feed the autonomous nervous systems, waking it up so to speak. A mindfulness exercise to bring you fully into your body after waking ensures that any traveling parts of you are welcomed back openly and closed around the full body in a warm embrace. We often think of our mornings as a time of dread. Starting in this way of warm embrace provides a strong comfort to all the systems, nourishing, loving, and calm. Orderly, in the sense that we must be fully present and together in order to be our most complete–in form and function.

Elements of routine that aid the body include washing the face three times with cold water to awaken the physical senses, standing firmly in tree pose to find our center, cleaning the rooms of excess energy released during the night by opening windows and doors, delaying any difficult conversations until we have adequately prepared our minds to be loving, compassionate and kind with only positive intentions.

The evening routine is equally meaningful. The return to our den is where we retreat for warmth, restoration, and peace. This should become the foundation of family periods, to regain connection, foster an exchange of mutual gratitude, feeding of the soul through food, music, and companionship. Making waves of warmth to those who cannot find their way. This is the period where their receptiveness is enhanced, thus able to receive this message clearer. Practices such as prayer, games, and movies connect us, in immediate space and beyond. This is where prayer at a meal and at night time originate from, gratitude and sharing of good intention to others. It was never meant to be a religious act of faith, yet powers that be defined it to their liking.

Prayer sends intention, good will, to all beings or to one who may need it most. Energy channeling during the physical incarnation towards others is through prayer. It is not a belief, it is an action of pure intent, of goodness, of the betterment in the whole. All is not lost on those who pray for themselves or of a God or system. Their message will be received at the vibration in which they dwell until their realization has begun. Ample time is afforded to try and try again.

Boundless determination makes up the rest of the day, holding in your intentions to provide goodness through service and actions, a compassionate heart, and loving kindness to self and others. Naturally one will ask how to achieve this state when you no longer wish to be striving at the place in which you are. It is simple. Afford yourself the compassion that your best possibility is finding its way to you. Rest in that knowing. And while you rest in that, seek the options and actions within your daily work that allow the highest goodness to take form. Within each task, there is a purpose and a positive action for you.

Determining the successful action only requires of you to *feel* the corresponding outcome. How does it feel? If there is discomfort, choose again until the option feels warm and true. If you must choose anything different choose a neutral feeling. Those feeling tactics are centered around your knowing of goodness and will always serve you well.

Reaching for the stars is one of the most important acts that we can provide our soul. A chance to dream, treating its journey here as one of its most important ventures. Because it is. To withhold opportunity or possibility greatly detaches us from our very existence, cutting us off from the very cosmic energy that created us. We are born from it and require its constant breath to fuel us into the direction of evolution. To stay in one place is to stagnate. A puddle in the absence of movement and replenishment becomes mirky, lacking the clarity and the vibrancy that it once was.

Navigating the waters of change may be the hardest process that humans have been able to master. We once were able to shift and move with the tides, adjust to the changing seasons, move to where food was abundant. We acknowledged the cycle of life and the deeper meaning to these changes. We were aware of the need to and did not resist. We flowed.

As we became centered in our structures–bricks and mortar, societies, places, belongings–we became more and more reluctant to change. First, in place, it became harder to move, and then in systems. They provided structure, stability, a sense of belonging. And so, we detached from the "place" (aka Earth) that we respected for its movement, to a different sort of "place" which is much different. Same, but not. We hold ourselves here, mainly for practical reasons, but it presents as a resistance.

When our highest possibility is "somewhere else" how do we move to it when the place cannot move to us? The saying goes, a sailboat which shifts course by only one degree will find himself in a very different place. This is how the place comes to us. Minor shifts can have a profound effect on how our daily lives change over time. And it's just enough to make space for possibilities and shift us out of resistance.

Chapter 18
Wishful Thinking

How might one get from A to B when there is no map, no instructions, no guideposts to be seen. Is it just wishful thinking that one day we will wake up and find ourselves where we belong? Not a chance. We must be willing to first open ourselves to change, see the new way of "seeing", watching for the signs that inevitably are there for us. Waking each day resting in the knowing and aligning with the knowing. It will be there, and we will make the adjustments that are guided along the way.

Remarkable things happen when you open yourself in this way. Signs and synchronicities are everywhere, yet we think us fools to believe such meaningless nonsense. How could those signs possibly be meant for us? This is how the Universe conspires *for* us, not against us. Always. It wants what you want. The highest and best. That is what will serve you, humanity, and the Universe.

Why must we deduce that the Universe is not so intelligent? Look around you. The things that have been created in your absence so that you could be present within it, fully supported in all ways in order for you to achieve your highest potential–irregardless of the play in evolutionary time you were to look. The Universe is conspiring for you, my dear one. There is no need to study it, analyze it, prove it. It is. And there is no way to disprove what just is.

Fancy you may one day like to take a train ride to Paris for your birthday? Why can that not be so? You will first run through all the reasons why you shouldn't, couldn't, and wouldn't. Do you think the Universe is thinking in this way? Nope. There is only one thing to register. The what and the intent. The what: a train ride to Paris. The why: to set your soul on fire. Give me one reason why the Universe would not see the goodness in a deserving soul being regenerated by an experience. There is a time and place, yes, and this means that what you ask may not materialize immediately. But it is registered. That wishful thinking–when framed by good intent, purpose, and alignment with soul–has all the ingredients to materialize into pure potential. The gift is in the timing.

There may be valid reason the Universe cannot deliver. In due time. And when time is already an illusion it will occur when it is due. Maybe there is generosity that must be afforded to the Universe to deliver on its requests. It has many to fulfill after all.

There is a kindness to wishful thinking. It is surrounded by a love for self, a deserving nature that we all are. Rather than being from a place of lack, the old adage of wishing for that which we cannot have, instead, consider it a "wish-fulfillment". Simply put–it is a "want fulfilled".

Credence must be given to those who aspire and do not back down from the knowing. Half of the battle is finding the knowing, so in a sense, you are already halfway there. Become your purpose. In every small way that you can. From many small actions there forms a much larger foundation for which your purpose can rest upon and flourish. There need not be effort, only purpose and intent. The ingredients will find their way to you.

Take a chance on yourself for a change. Be willing to see yourself as the light that you are. How can others see it if you cannot see it yourself? As with the regeneration of our aura in the night, our daily habits and thoughts can deplete or change its frequency. Thus, diminishing our ability to see our own light. Striving to fill our cup daily with the little things in life that bring us joy will at least keep the fire from going out before we stumble upon the knowing.

It is here, in the fading light that one must be most open to change in order to allow the field of possibility to open around you. It is then, the first feeling of the knowing, that will make its greatest impression upon you. There is no unknowing the knowing after that point. You have been found.

Chapter 19
Unbreakable

We delve in the depths of our soul not to see how broken we are, rather how unbreakable we are. While there may be parts of ourselves awaiting to be seen, hinged to a story of another place and time, we are not broken. In fact, we proceed in life without that place, making the best of it that we can. Sure, we have less balance and more challenge to overcome. However, we are not broken. **We are unbreakable if we see into the magic that we truly are.**

Our bodies can define our age in this human body but cannot define *how* we live. We can expressly have an immediate impact on our daily life when we can see and value our interconnectedness as an individual being–our internal systems that function to support us–and its web of systems external to us. Fractured maybe at times, but never broken. We can heal those fractures if we offer it the love and compassion that it needs to mend.

Mending a broken flame needs only two things. A breath of fresh air and fuel to keep it alive. By fresh air, meaning clarity, coherence, and confidence to step into yourself again, your worthiness to be alive and do great things. Fuel must be of the living kind. An aliveness rich in pure free energy, without energetic disturbance. Food free of processing. Thoughts freed from limitations.

Anything that inspires pure joy can turn a match with no wood into a blazing fire driven simply from that joy. Resounding laughter can be the best medicine, bringing fresh air deep within the lungs, a space that typically gets cut off from oxygen as our breathing becomes shallow during times of stress or constriction. It lifts the clouds just high enough to see ourselves in the mirror, unwilling to be blown out quite yet. It inspires us. It respires us anew.

Juggling the awakening process with daily living and keeping the flame alive and well can place considerable demands on our energy. Changing how we spend our time can lead to either improved states of mind or feelings of defeat. To be inspired by our flame but not replenished enough to sustain it can lead to frustration and a reluctance to fully give in to the process. It is imperative that you attempt at least for a significant period to self-reflect on your needs, options, and ways to incorporate more rest and self-care during the process. This will look differently to all, depending on your base level of energy, mood, and disposition.

Take the time at each moment it is offered. Be observant of signs of depletion and be sure to avoid running low for too long or too often. Seek others to help in moving through the process. Energy healers, biofeedback specialists, and massage therapy all help to move energy through the body, physical or energetic. Many offer the additional insight where the practitioner is clairvoyant or clairaudient and can bring forward information that the energy holds. These modalities will be your primary for healing.

Once you are in a restful state, able to accommodate the waves of energy moving in and out of you, you will realize how unbreakable you are. The ability for your mind and body to relive such traumas, ancestral or current life, and be returned more whole and light is just one piece of strength that will continually lead you further and further on your path. To reach higher and higher states of wholeness, of lightness, will relieve the density that has dragged us down for generations. Freeing, resilient. Comprised of only love for our self, our selves, and the whole.

Remembering the story of our truest self, owning our choices, and finding a new way to live. **At the core is that this journey is meant for us and us alone, to do so in our own way and pace.** We are never forced, only guided down a path that will support our greatest potential. In harmony this is done, not to say in the absence of challenge and monumental upheavals. Rather the harmony is the reconciling of our current state with our truest state. To gain harmony, we must practice over and over again.

There is a story once told of the man who would lay awake, asking for guidance from all that would listen. He waited and he waited. He did not understand why there was never a response, kind gesture, or a helping hand. He was answered one night when no one was around. It was his voice. You have the answers. Why are you asking out there?

We each have guides and spirits available to us, but our most important guide is the one within us. The one keeping us together no matter how broken we may feel. It waits patiently for us to ask it, acknowledge its presence. When the time comes it will respond.

And when it does, what will you do? Will you continue to see value in those around you or can you offer your ear to the voice that knows you the most? To the internal one, allowing you to live as you have, fumbling, foibling, destructive at times. The one who has watched you take your first breath, walked you to school, nudged you to make a different decision, cheered you on when you thought you had no more to give. This voice is paramount. It leads you every step of the way.

Ask for it.

Listen to it.

Follow it.

It will never steer you wrong. It is your *intuition*, your inner voice, inner compass–whatever you wish to call it. Abide by it. In sickness and in health, it is there for you and only you. No one else.

There will come a time when you find that your decisions become easier when you allow this inner voice to speak. From what is best for your morning meal, the choice of clothes that influence how you want to feel, the daily routine, the life-changing decisions, and most importantly what is best for you at any given moment of the day.

Each moment, each step can be guided. If you happen to veer off course, the silent whisper does so respectfully in the hopes that you will recognize the diversion. And when you don't, that whisper shall roar. For it is serving you and only the highest and best will do. Nothing less.

And always remember, this is all for you. Be willing to take yourself to new heights. You won't know what you will find until you get there. And it may be beyond your wildest dreams.

Chapter 20
Where Art Thou

Frame yourself as art. A majestic masterpiece that is meant to be seen and shown in the world. Meant to be observed and digested in a showroom of all your glory for their eyes to see. Relinquish all notions that you have come here to do anything. Rest. Rest on that wall gently, safely, keeping a watchful eye. There is only one thing to do. Be amongst the masses. Receive what is rightfully yours and give back what is theirs to keep in a new and reformed way.

There is a light in your eyes that can see through the trauma, the pain, and suffering right down to the core of their being. There is a light that transfers to the core and rebuilds the sense of purpose from the inside out despite the layers upon layers that must be healed in due time. The spark must be there initially and fostered. The more people that can foster the light transmission the more likely there is to be a wide enough awakening to shift the scales back to where they belong.

Marking progress towards balance is the responsibility of the gatekeepers, those that hold accountable our principles and values, and whether they are diminishing or growing to a sufficient state for change to take place. The gatekeepers will record and transmit new instructions for the Second Coming of Christ if the growth is not at a pace which can keep up with the evolutionary requirements and enlightenment path. We are all heading there, but the pace at which we are at requires a massive shift to reorder the stages of the future.

There cannot be willful improvement with the current lack of awareness and acknowledgment of Universal Laws that govern this universe. Complete diminishing of those laws is not an option. Hindering evolution is not an option. Enlightenment is not a quest for power over others, it is for power of the whole.

Digging deep into the soul is like excavating for diamonds. Sometimes you find a gold mine. While others it is a glimpse, a glimmer of something so distant, yet it feels known, akin to seeing your mate for the first time. Knowing them, from some far-off distant place or time. It is the glimmer that has the most profound effect on us.

It sets us seeking, inquiring for the deeper purpose and meaning of all of this. It gives us hope of miracles, of divine intervention, and interludes with God, or the higher power we may believe in. It reaches the recesses of our mind that have remained untouched, or so we had thought. For there is no part of our mind or physical body that remains untouched in the evolutionary process. There are hidden elements within us waiting to be seen, ordained in light, activating us to set us free. Beyond limits. Unbound by time or place as we are now.

Our next existence may not be hard if we right the wrongs of our past. Greater freedom, fluidity, resonance, happiness that we strive for. It is within our grasp if we choose it so. Beings of light is what we are. There is no other explanation that science can logically provide. And with light, we are malleable, untenable, elevated to new heights when we lay down our burdens, our guards, our strife and limiting tendencies. The body's limits are only those that we impose on it.

Practice being of light. A conduit of energy for yourself and the people around you. Treasure this light, as if it were gold. You achieve this light through perseverance and dedication to your spirit and it must not be taken lightly. There are beings that will naturally gravitate to you in order to seek your light. Doing this will signal to their body when they are ready, the same remembering that was experienced upon your awakening. The power of your light is immense and has the potential to put in play a ripple effect of awakening simply by being in their presence.

The notion of being more than doing is paramount at this time. Expanding the scales of goodness, reclaiming one's power, generating sufficient vibrancy to reconnect with one's most highest self and inner power, are all driven by centering oneself consistently and permanently.

To permanently center oneself, you must rid the body of all that it isn't. Beliefs, thoughtforms, negative emotions bound within various parts of the body, muscle tissue, fascia, skeletal system, endocrine system—all must be removed. These negative emotions have a tendency to sway our center in the direction of harm towards self. One must seek always actions that are for the good of self.

Self-love is not just about compassion and caretaking of the body. It is the primary means of discerning that which will give goodness to self *and* others, or only for others. Self-love can be determinantal to ourselves if its only purpose is to be able to maintain the serving function to others and in a manner that does not consider the soul. Martyrdom is self-harm in the respect that it absolves our own soul's needs in an attempt to seek others' happiness.

Selfishness, on the other hand, provides no goodness for others and centers one's actions in the interest of self over others. **The purpose of self-love is for the whole—to remain in one's highest capacity to serve for the good of our own purpose *and* that of others.**

Along the same vein, is the elimination of structures that bind us in the opposite direction of where we need to go. The constructs of society—schooling, careers, family—all which historically have been devoid of spirit and applying one's knowing. This will require creativity as society is not yet ready to relinquish these *en masse*, and in the absence of those individuals awakening, it will take time.

Choices that can be made include how one chooses to enable their purpose during the course of their day, the practices that enable spirit to remain strong and supported, the way in which we instill fundamental concepts of consciousness within the family unit and the schooling, enabling informed choice of our youngest generations, and avoiding the detachment from spirit that typically occurs in the early years.

When we return into our bodies, fully and completely as spirit and as human form we welcome back our true essence of who we are, from day one. Not our birth, but our presence as spirits to earth. We have come here to learn, to speak our truths, to be whole in all our forms, and to overcome the nature of the human mind.

Observing pattern and feeling are the two most particular traits we have that can help our existence. Only us humans can do so, despite the intelligence of other beings namely the animals of high intelligence. But these are the ones closest to us. As humans, we are the only ones capable of destroying the earth with our own bare hands. We make our destiny as mankind and our soul's journey. We have the ability, but only when we use our intelligence correctly, in its purest form, and with purest intentions.

Then we shall transcend.

Then we shall see the power of our hearts to unite as a collective consciousness even further together.

All functioning as one. In harmony.

The End.

Recommended Practices: Book One

Connect to your inner voice and intuition

- Find a space where you can remain in peace and undisturbed quiet for a minimum of 72 hours.

Resolve your fears

- See and hear them, truly and deeply.

- What is causing turmoil within yourself? Pay yourself attention to what requires attention. Regularly. It gnaws because it is important.

- Help other souls remember their light, especially during dark times.

Create and nurture the container for the soul to speak

- Presence, calmness, and a willingness to look inside. BE, fully, and completely, with no demands, no distractions, and no recurring pain. Allow for healing.

- Support efficient functioning of the systems in the lower third of the body (womb, stomach, spleen, and intestines).

- Consume bone broth regularly.

- Breathwork, yoga, and space to be in-body.

- Access your guides and angels regularly.

Shedding and releasing phases

Allow the soul to retract, regenerate, integrate, and alleviate what no longer serves the highest needs.

- Withdraw from daily activities, resume activities when guided and appropriate.

- Lay on a comfortable platform or bed to support stillness.

- Consume pure foods in bright colors to move energy to lighter realms and support digestion.

- Consume warming foods and elixirs to stimulate digestion and heat the body.

- Minimize heavy tasks or activities.

Intention of the whole

- When taking individual action, bring true intention of the whole.

- Individual strength supports the whole. You cannot give from an empty cup.

The weight of the past

- The past is to be learned from not to stay in.

Change beliefs

- Daily, identify where a change in belief needs to occur for the highest good. Bring light to this intention and hold it throughout the day. Walk with it and the place will find you.

Harness kundalini energy

Once per month initially, then once per week maximum, allowing for integration in between. Nurture the soul and physical body during this process, eliminate all toxins and reducing environments. Regularly rest and use relaxation techniques, consume bright foods and beverages, and apply subtle acupressure on the forehead. Resist the urge to process too deeply. Establish a meditation practice in advance.

1. Bring the body and mind to complete stillness and non-thought.

2. Imagine a cord connecting you to the earth's core. Bring earth force into the root chakra and samsidara chakra embedded within. Observe pressure across the pelvic region. Bring this pressure up the main channel across the remaining chakras. When the crown is reached, grasp the skies with your mind's eye, remaining connected with the earth.

3. With upper and lower chakras connected and spinning, envision a powerful light at the base of the spine where it meets the coccygeal region. Use white light to stimulate the region. Maintain safety and presence. Observe the circuit proceed up the spine. Observe visions, feelings, sensations.

Allow what needs to rise and release

- Do not engage the temptations linked to the events. Observe, breathe, and release until it is no longer visible within your mind or body.

- Remain calm and centered to create safety in the nervous system, usurp the fight or flight system to establish a new process that recognizes the sensitivity of the body and deep rooted knowing in the soul.

Ask the basic questions

- Is this my soul speaking?

- Is this true of my soul?

- What does my soul want?

Recommended Practices: Book Two

Connect to your dharma/purpose daily

- Hold this essence throughout your day and activities.

Create symbiosis of the body systems

- Remove irritants from the diet and skincare.

- Nourish at the cellular and muscular level: eat leafy green vegetables daily, warming foods (soups stews) and less cold salads at dinner, and equal portions of carbohydrates and proteins.

- Soothe the spirit with restful activities (baths, meditate, linger, journal).

- Balance effort with tranquility through Yoga, Pilates, and meandering-type walking.

- Allow any emotions or sensations to come through.

Establish a daily routine

- Morning: wash the face three times with cold water and mindfully stimulate the scalp when showering, welcoming back any traveling parts of you. Center the body in Vrksasana tree pose. Open windows and doors to clear the air. Delay difficult conversations until the mind is prepared for love, compassion, kindness, and positive intention.

- Evening: establish a foundation of family connection, gratitude, and feeding the soul (food, music, games, movies, and companionship).

- Before sleep: meditate to allow for processing and releasing of the day's events. Avoid guided meditations or meditations that expand without recentering inside the body.

Option A or Option B Test

- Sit quietly and centered in your heart. Bring your awareness to Option A. How does it feel within your body? Does your body want to open and expand, or contract into itself? Does it feel warm or is there aggravation or aversion somewhere in the body?

- Apply the same process to Option B and any other options.

- Which one feels most loving and expansive within the body?

Prayer

- Send intention, good will, to all beings or to one who may need it most.

Practice being of light

- Imagine yourself as a conduit of energy. Treasure this light as if it were gold.

- Remain dedicated to your spirit.

- Frame yourself as art. Rest, be seen, observe, receive, and give back.

Permanently center yourself

- Rid the body of all that it isn't: beliefs, thoughtforms, negative emotions.

- Identify where these exist within the body (muscle tissue, fascia, skeletal system, endocrine system) and use relevant modalities to release them.

Choose actions of goodness: of self, the family unit, and youngest generations.

- Does it enable my purpose during the course of the day?

- Does it enable the spirit to remain strong and supported?

- Does it instill attachment to spirit? Does it prevent detaching from spirit?

- Does it instill consciousness within the family unit and

the schooling?

- Do actions for self-love foster my highest capacity for the good of my purpose *and* that of others?

- Observing the patterns and feelings, do they contribute to or detract from growth, expansion, and living in truth?

About the Author

Valentina M. Grosvenor, a conscious channeler on a journey of self-discovery and self-actualization, is guided by the spirit world and helps others on their journey home to themselves. Awakening to a new world, life events have paved the way on her spiritual path to unveil her hidden gifts and life purpose. Through willing openness and observation, she holds a deep faith and trust in the wisdom that unfolds, day by day, moment by moment. Like a flower meticulously revealing its delicate, vibrant petals one by one, ever so beautifully and in perfect form with the world around her.